Make a Memory!

NOT WITHOUT MY FATHER:
ONE WOMAN'S 444-MILE WALK
OF THE NATCHEZ TRACE

ANDRA WATKINS

WORD HERMIT PRESS LLC

Not Without My Father: One Woman's 444-Mile Walk of the Natchez Trace is a memoir. It chronicles the author's actual experiences with real places and people. Some identities and locations are disguised or combined. The author's father's narration is a product of the author's imagination.

ISBN-13: 978-0-9908593-1-4

LIBRARY OF CONGRESS CATALOG NUMBER APPLIED FOR

Not Without My Father

One Woman's 444-Mile Walk of the Natchez Trace

NOTE ON THE STRUCTURE OF THE MEMOIR

This is a memoir.
And it isn't.
My narration is my voice. My experience. My truth.
My father's narration (*in italics*) is comprised of his stories. Some as he tells them. Others as I imagine them.
The chapter titles are a playlist of road music and walking songs. If you spend 34 days walking 444 miles, you need a soundtrack to keep you company.

Not Without My Father

DEDICATION

For my father
Roy Lee Watkins, Junior

And in memory of Jeffrey Lee Nelson
March 10, 1957 - July 10, 2014
A father taken from his family too soon

Not Without My Father

BOOKS BY ANDRA WATKINS

Non-fiction

Not Without My Father: One Woman's 444-Mile Walk of the Natchez Trace
(January 2015)

Photography

Natchez Trace: Tracks in Time
(March 2015)

Fiction

To Live Forever: An Afterlife Journey of Meriwether Lewis
(March 2014)

Not Without My Father

MAP OF THE NATCHEZ TRACE

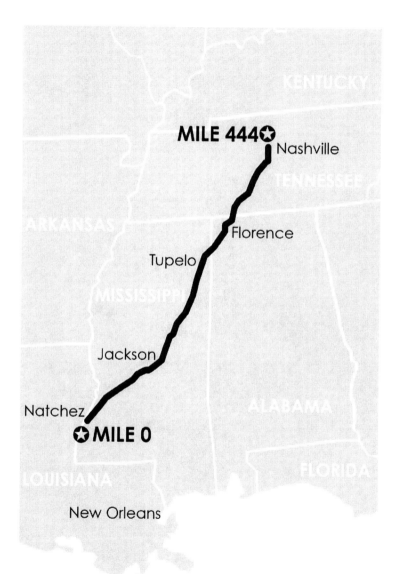

Not Without My Father

ROAD TO NOWHERE

Talking Heads

The journey is a long slog with an unpredictable number of mileposts. One can make the trip alone, but why not share it?

As I traversed familiar mile markers and pulled up in front of my father's house, I could predict where I'd find him.

In his recliner, his belly a shelf for a vat of popcorn. At eighty, he whiled away days feeding his face and shouting at the television. Whenever his throne was vacant, I eschewed all temptation to occupy it.

Because I imagined how many times he farted into the velvet upholstery.

Sometimes while naked.

I could hear the television when I stepped from the car. "Why am I doing this again?" I whispered as I slipped through the back door.

"Andra!" There he was, sprawled in his recliner. A jagged scar played peek-a-boo through his open pajama top. "What're you doing here?"

I opened my mouth and clamped it shut. Once I uttered my request, I couldn't take it back.

I needed a wingman while I walked the 444-mile Natchez Trace from Natchez, Mississippi to Nashville, Tennessee. I planned to launch my debut novel and become the first living person to walk the 10,000-year-old road as our ancestors did. Nobody could convince me

that an unathletic woman and her mid-life paunch were incapable of walking more than a half-marathon every day for a month.

Even though my aversion to exercise was as spectacular as my father's.

I wanted my walk to redeem my novel's hero, American explorer Meriwether Lewis, one-half of the Lewis and Clark duo. He died of two gunshot wounds on the Natchez Trace, seventy miles south of Nashville.

He was only thirty-five.

Was it suicide? Or murder? His death is one of America's great unsolved mysteries.

To walk a forgotten highway for five weeks, I needed a wingman who could shuttle me to my first daily milepost and pick me up fifteen miles later. Someone who wasn't busy. Someone available. Maybe this person even craved an adventure.

I scrolled through a list of prospects. My husband Michael couldn't be absent from work for five weeks, especially since his job paid for my predilection to write. My friends all had children. Husbands. Gainful employment. I discarded people for an hour, my list a scribbled mess that highlighted one harrowing name.

Dad.

My father wasn't doing anything. He was available to go on a five-week jaunt through Mississippi, Alabama and Tennessee.

His stomach pooled over his thighs and his triple-chin jiggled as he leaned into his response. "Go on a five-week trip? Just you and me? I don't want to do that, Andra."

"Why not?" I shouted even louder to penetrate his VA-issued, circa-1980 hearing aids.

"Well." He chewed a handful of popcorn. "Because.......I got furniture to refinish."

"It'll be here when you get back."

Dad dug his fingernails into the arms of his chair. "I cain't be away from my Sunday school class for that long."

"God won't care if you miss church to spend time

with your only daughter, Dad."

"Well, uh.......I........Linda might need me here."

Mom preened into the room with his bowl of ice cream. I never understood why she didn't just hand him the carton. She placed the spoon between his fingers and smiled. "I don't need you here, Roy." Her flawless makeup matched her leotard. "I'm going to the gym. Be home in four hours."

She flounced out the door, leaving me with my jiggly arms and red hair I forgot to brush.

I sighed and turned back to Dad. "Why don't you want to do this, Dad? I mean, you haven't been anywhere since your appendix ruptured two years ago. You're just sitting here in this recliner, waiting to die."

Dad picked at his ice cream and avoided my gaze. "Spending five weeks with you don't sound like much fun, Andra."

Dad and I shouted down my teens, harangued through my twenties and seethed away my thirties. For most of my life, our every interaction disintegrated into hurtful words and pregnant silences. Yet, I was willing to cast our history aside and endure his company for more than a month, while he rejected me?

Wrong answer, Old Man.

I gnawed my tongue to regroup. Dad was my last hope to take readers into my book's world. To help my scribblings make me somebody. In a universe of words with little meaning and even less point, I believed I created something valuable, a story that could make a difference, a tale that would leave readers fundamentally altered and pining for the next installment.

All writers are convinced whatever they write qualifies, be it dreck or brilliance. Our words are sperm and egg on the page. Merge them together, and one can hold a physical chunk of the writer. It's a shame a book can't arrive covered in blood and filth from the birth canal, screaming and howling to breathe.

But to get anyone to care about a story, the writer must make it about the reader.

My breathing even, I flashed my most fetching smile.

"All right, Dad. Look at it this way. We'll be riding near hundreds of tiny towns with lots of strangers who've never heard your stories. Think of all the junk shops and dive diners where you can enchant people. Don't they deserve to meet you before you're gone?"

Dad's eyes took on a dreamy tinge. His yarns were Southern gothic legends, tales he rolled out for every stranger he encountered. I imagined myself spending the entire trip with a view of his broad back, regaling everyone but me. He must've conjured the same scene. "I'll do it, Andra. If the Lord lets me live 'til March, I'll go with you."

Dad would be my wingman on the Natchez Trace. Visions of literary stardom floated in front of my faraway eyes. Because my secret dream was *The New York Times* headline:

- *Debut Novelist Walks Her Way to Blockbuster Best Seller!* -

I basked in the mirage of that proclamation, in the glory of staggering to my Nashville finish line with crowds of people. News crews. Fans waving my book and clamoring for an autograph.

My swelling imagination burst when Dad heaved himself from the chair, scratched his crotch and farted. "Yeah, Andra. This is gonna be real fun."

What had I done? Besides self-scratching and legendary gas, his sleep apnea machine didn't stifle his explosive snoring.

And the bathroom. I would have to share a bathroom with my father, whose hulking belly obscured all ability to aim. A sodden fact that seeped into my legs when I locked myself in Dad's bathroom and plopped down on the toilet.

I didn't want to spend five weeks with my father.

As I winced through a sink bath, I studied my face in the mirror. The beginnings of forehead wrinkles and crows feet. A hint of Dad's bulldog  jowl. I stuck my tongue out at my green-eyed self. "Welcome to Hell, you idiot."

HIT THE ROAD JACK
Ray Charles

Dad moseyed through the faded grandeur of the Plantation Suite at Hope Farm, a bed and breakfast in Natchez, Mississippi. Our first stop on my 444-mile Natchez Trace Parkway saga. Dad planted himself between two canopied beds. "That the TV?" It was the size of an iPad, perched on a desk. He fumbled with his suspenders and rocked back and forth on the Persian rug, eyeing chairs he knew wouldn't hold his weight. "How'm I gonna watch that?"

I left him cradling his sleep apnea machine and followed my friend Alice into Mississippi dusk. "What am I doing here?" I whispered.

"You're gonna be the first person to walk the Natchez Trace as the pioneers did." Alice slammed the trunk of Dad's tan Mercury Grand Marquis and pushed her glasses up the bridge of her nose. My dearest friend was the ballast that would protect me from the onslaught of my father's outsized personality.

Alice had been part of my life for more than a decade. In my early thirties, my friends were all married, including Alice. I was the only pathetic single person I knew. While everyone talked about the possibility of babies, percolating babies and actual, birthed-and-breathing babies, I chewed my lip and wondered if I'd ever meet a functional man and contemplate babies.

Or maybe I wasn't functional.

I sat alone in my house, ate alone at my table, showered alone in my bathroom, and slept alone in my bed; yet, I didn't want to be alone.

I endured lunches and dinners, drinks and parties, listening to everyone compare notes on the next phase of life, a milestone I couldn't achieve. They wove their stories on blue-lined notebook paper, while I clung to holes in the margin. I came away from these interactions, my insides shrunken and my life an afterthought. I thought nobody cared about me.

Except Alice.

Even though she was pregnant herself, she tried to steer group conversations to non-gestational topics. "What books are you reading?" She asked. Or, "Tell me about your last trip." One time, she interrupted someone mid-ultrasound photo essay. "We've been talking about pregnancy for almost an hour. Can we spend the last few minutes of lunch on something else?"

If friends are a reflection of who we want to be, I wanted to be more like Alice.

While I wove from thing to thing to thing in a vain effort to find myself, she became partner in an architecture firm and mothered a daughter I considered a niece. She was primary caregiver to her disabled brother and supreme supporter of her husband. I cultivated a friendship with her, because I wanted to be her. I never understood how she did everything, but I thought if I got to know her better, some of her juju would dribble onto me.

A decade on, she was a seminal figure in my life.

Alice and I decided Dad as wingman would be the equivalent of what writers call an unreliable narrator. He might intend to drop me off and pick me up each day, but given the wealth of strangers between miles one and fifteen, he couldn't be depended upon to be there for me.

Alice agreed to babysit my father and schlep me around for the first week of my Natchez Trace walk. The rest would be just Dad and me.

I didn't want to think about that.

Not yet.

I shoved the looming time with my father over my shoulder in a moon-lit parking lot. If I thought about what was coming, I'd quit before I took one step.

Alice heaved grocery bags up narrow stairs. "I think that's everything you'll need for a long walk."

"Maybe." I held the screen door and followed her into our suite. A jumble of athletic gear awaited me. Compression tights. Hiking shoes. Energy bars. CamelBak water bladder. Gadgets and creams designed for the extreme athlete.

An athlete? Who was I kidding? In high school, I couldn't run a mile, score a goal or hit a ball. Why did I think I could walk more than a half-marathon every day for a month at forty-four?

I spread a map across the quilted bedspread. A long rectangle stretched from one side of the bed to the other.

The Natchez Trace.

Almost 450 miles of highway ringed by farms and swampland, its sides were eroded canyons in some places. Ghostly buffalo herds competed with the earliest Native American spirits, Spanish conquistadors, French missionaries and warring armies along a paved federal parkway. I imagined their voices, and I honored them in my novel. Ten thousand years of history.

The Trace was a tunnel through Time.

From March 1 to April 3, 2014, I planned to walk the highway as our ancestors did. Fifteen miles a day. One rest day a week. For thirty-four days.

On the eve of my start, I perused a daunting list of things to do: Stock up on snacks for my daily food kit; buy enough bottled water; organize supplies for easy access as we moved; fall asleep early to be rested. I flitted between piles of stuff, wondering how I would winnow it into one compact pack. I read Cheryl Strayed's *Wild*, about her trek up the Pacific Crest Trail. I didn't want to carry unnecessary things.

Food, a water-filled CamelBak, Gatorade, a first-aid kit, extra socks, flashlight, toilet paper, waterproof pants, a spare battery pack for my iPhone, cards announcing my novel, notes from readers, a Parkway map, a voodoo doll and mace. Items of necessity. Charms for good luck. One weapon. Two if the voodoo doll counted.

Everything I needed.

I flattened a roll of toilet paper and shoved it into a ziplock bag. "Dad, can you help me go through this list? Check off things as I call them out? Dad?"

Even though Dad wore hearing aids, I had to shout if I wanted him to hear me. He said they didn't pick up children and women with higher voices, but I caught him turning them off around me. I barreled into the other room and found Dad standing in front of a precarious bureau, his sleep apnea machine balanced on a ledge. An electrical cord dangled from one hand. "Dad! Help me here?"

"I cain't find a place to plug this thing up." His filmy eyes scanned walls papered with yellowed clippings of Dwight Eisenhower and Barry Goldwater. "This all seems like yesterday……"

I groped along the walls and felt an outlet behind the bed. "You can plug it right here." I picked up the end of the cord and scooted under the bed. When I stuck the prongs in the socket, I held my breath. "No telling whether the wiring in this place is up to code, right Dad?" Silence. "Oh well, maybe he can't hear me under here." Layers of history peeled back with me as I heaved myself to stand. Coughing, I knocked dust from my knees in the empty room. "Dad?"

I opened the bathroom door, expecting to find Dad spraying everything but the toilet, but it was vacant. Foiled, I darted into the other room. "Where's Dad?"

Alice reclined on one of two mountainous canopy beds, blonde hair splayed on the pillow. Her eyes drooped behind glasses perched on her heart-shaped face, and her voice ran thick like syrup. "He went over to talk to Miss Ethel."

"Again? Jesus God, it's after nine o'clock."

She punched her pillow and settled onto her side. "I guess she's the only stranger he can find to talk to at this time of night, Andra."

Miss Ethel was the doyenne of Hope Farm, a spunky wisp of a woman in her seventies. When I checked in earlier that afternoon, she met me at the front door and blinked through thick glasses. "Surely you're not gonna walk all the way to Nashville, Ondra?"

I winced and bit my lip when she butchered my name, but I didn't correct her. People usually didn't get it, even when I smiled and said, "It's AN-dra."

Miss Ethel fingered her double string of pearls, her wrinkled face unreadable. "Well. Bless your heart. My Yankee husband'll be sorry he died before he could meet the likes of you." She swooshed one silk-clad arm. "Allow me to escort you to your room." I followed the impressions her black pumps made in the carpet.

Hours later, I looked at the clock on my phone and slipped my feet into some sneakers. "I have a sick feeling I'm seeing what my father was like when he was courting women."

Information no child, little or grown, wants to know.

Not Without My Father

KING OF THE ROAD
Roger Miller

I wandered along the sloping veranda to the front house. Miss Ethel's house. Crickets chirped a symphony in the garden. Through a portal of wavy glass, I spied on my father. His balloon stomach strained the integrity of a wooden side chair in Miss Ethel's den. If I shifted to the left, I glimpsed her helmet of light brown hair bobbing over the back of the sofa. I could identify his stories by the hand gestures he used.

Acres of Biscuits bled into Hot Shot to become the ridiculous Butterbean Song.

"Dad!" I pushed through the door, chords of laughter still lingering in the chilly air. "I got your machine working, and—"

"Andra!" Miss Ethel's Mississippi drawl stretched my name to three syllables. "I'm sorry I got your name wrong. Roy here was just telling me you were named after Andra Willis. Is that right?"

Dad cackled. "Yeah. Andra Willis. That singer on the Lawrence Welk Show."

Miss Ethel slapped one knee. "Why in the world would you name your daughter after a woman on the Lawrence Welk Show, Roy?"

"Linda liked the name Leslie Lynn, but I didn't know no Leslie Lynns. I sure did like that Andra Willis, though. Every time she sang, I made sure to watch. She was real

pretty. I never got tired of looking at her, and—"

"Dad! Ew! I don't want to stand here and listen to you tell Miss Ethel about how you named me after some woman you thought was hot."

"I still see her sometimes. On them re-runs."

While Dad nursed his lust, Miss Ethel turned to me. "Anyway, do you really mean to walk all the way to Nashville, Andra?"

Her question pushed me into a chair along the far wall. How many months had I thought about walking the Trace? Five? Ten?

Four days a week for three months, I trained near my Charleston, South Carolina home. I trudged across the concrete bridge that spanned Charleston's harbor and pounded my feet into the pavement of the West Ashley Greenway. During a winter storm, I zipped myself into rain gear and let the wind blow me around Charleston's Battery.

I spent weeks planning my route, measuring the distance between locations in my novel, deciding how to make them interesting to potential readers, and coordinating the publicity that would make my story a commercial success.

Innumerable times, I wanted to quit, but my husband Michael told me I could do it. He often rode alongside me on his bicycle, cheering me onward. When people asked why he was letting me walk, he replied, "You obviously don't know my wife."

I prepared myself physically. I studied every detail of the terrain. I had the most supportive husband alive.

I was ready.

When morning dawned, my book would have its official birthday, and my father would celebrate with me.

Because he challenged me to make something of myself, nagging me into epic arguments. I wasn't sure how I felt about having him along to  witness my one valiant attempt, because I failed at everything else. Certified public accountant? It left no room for creativity. Managing a multi-million dollar company? I decamped with the beginnings of an ulcer. At forty-four, I was a decade into my third career as a management consultant. The 2008 crash shriveled my earnings from six figures to under $10,000 in less than twelve months. I woke up at mid-life, the peak of my income potential, with no clients and no prospects. No one was hiring, especially when the applicant was a middle-aged Southern woman.

If I excelled at anything, it was failure.

I launched my walk online to thousands of readers as a public dare to myself, to prove I could do something audacious.

Life-long doubt assailed me. What if I couldn't finish? Or nobody read the book? If Dad and I couldn't stop fighting, what would I do?

I couldn't answer Miss Ethel through the obstruction in my throat. Instead, I fingered wooden arms and studied carpet patterns. In another room, a clock marked Time.

Time!

"Dad, you've got to let Miss Ethel go to bed. It's late."

Dad ignored me and revved the engine of memory. "Did I ever tell you—"

"I fixed your sleep apnea machine, and—"

Miss Ethel's laugh bisected our routine. "Has Roy ever told you he was a mistake?"

"I'm beginning to think this whole trip was a mistake," I mumbled but still turned to my father. Baited. "What mistake, Dad?"

"Well. After my mother had your Aunt Lillian, the doctor told her she wouldn't be able to have no more children. She was too tore up and all. You know, inside." The chair groaned when he shifted his weight. "That's why there's so much age difference. Seven years between me and my older sister. Good thing my parents still liked each other after all that time, I guess." Loose skin jangled when he laughed. "My mother always called me her miracle baby. 'Course, I was her only boy."

I rested my elbows on my knees to halt the spin of the room. A new Roy story. One I hadn't heard five billion times.

The clock chimed ten. As the music faded, I clucked, "I always knew you were a mistake, Dad."

"Yep. Wasn't ever supposed to be ole Roy."

Which meant I was even more miraculous. How many people made nothing of the miracle of Life?

Life had to smile on me, because I was trying to make something of the miracle.

"Let me tell you about that time—"

"Dad, Miss Ethel needs to—"

"—I was working with my father in the back field, and—"

"Dad!" I hurried over and stood between him and Miss Ethel. He talked through me while I pried him from the chair. I forced him to say goodnight and herded him along the starlit walkway to our shared suite. A breeze rippled the bed canopy as I listened to him use the toilet with the door open and swab a brush across browned teeth. The bed protested when he climbed between the covers, and a wet chorus of breathing sounds started less than a minute later. On the last night of February 2014, I lay in the dark and tried to obliterate the noise of my sleeping father.

"Your dad's going to be okay, Andra." Alice's voice penetrated the murky room.

I rolled on my side. "You don't have to whisper. He can't hear you." The weight of his every breath pressed into my chest. "I mean.....I'm sorry. Bad habit, joking when you're trying to be serious. I didn't realize how much he can't do anymore."

"But he's excited about this adventure. I can tell from watching him. That'll pull him through. That and how much he loves you."

"Oh, I don't know about that, the whole Dad-loving-me part. I mean, I know he loves me, but he doesn't say it much. Never has, really. I thought.........." I let my words dwindle into the crisp Mississippi night. Maybe I could finally figure out who my father was. Being together all the time might force us to talk, instead of cracking jokes and telling stories and yelling at each other.

I rearranged the bedspread to gather my courage, to clear tears clogging my throat. "Well. All I can say is I hope he makes it through tomorrow without falling down stairs or peeing his pants."

"He doesn't want me to leave you to walk alone."

I sat up and threw my legs over the side of the bed. My feet dangled above the floor like I lounged at the end of a pier. "But we've talked about this. There's no need for you to follow me for fifteen miles in the car when you could be out seeing pretty places around Natchez."

"I tried to tell him that."

"And?"

The bed squeaked, and Alice was framed in a square of window light. I strained to see her face. "He's really worried about you, Andra. He's afraid something will happen. Fifteen miles along a lonely Southern highway. A woman. Alone. Unarmed. It's like an engraved invitation for crazies."

"You know I have mace.....oh, wait. Don't tell Dad that."

"Why not?"

"He thinks I have a gun, and I don't want him to know what I have, because he'll tell people. He can't keep a secret."

"All I can say is I don't know whether he'll let me leave you in the morning. He's pretty damn determined."

I thought about Miss Ethel's breakfast ritual. The morning meal at Hope Farm always happened at 8:30am sharp. While we sipped coffee and nibbled bacon, Miss Ethel wove yarns that bested any storyteller in the room. Even my father. She entertained everyone all through breakfast, followed by a mandatory tour of the house. Miss Ethel's rules.

I jolted off the bed. "The tour!"

"What about it? "

"The tour will be how we'll get Dad to stay here in the morning. We can beg off because of my schedule. You know, slip out right after breakfast, and you can take me to start my walk."

"Do you think Miss Ethel will mind?"

"I'll talk to her first thing. Roy Lee Watkins will not miss a tour that promises priceless antique relics. Especially if he thinks he might know more about them than she does."

I leaped onto the towering bed as Dad's sleep machine crackled. Alice settled into her pillows and sighed. "I hope you're right, Andra. I hope you're right."

WALK THIS WAY
Aerosmith

When Dad followed Miss Ethel to the grand entrance of Hope Farm the next morning, Alice and I tiptoed through the kitchen. I lingered at the back door, listening to Miss Ethel describe her shock at the pricelessness of the urns on her mantle. "A museum curator from New Orleans almost had a stroke when he saw magnolia branches in those things. 'But they're vases' I told him. He mopped his brow with a hankie and retorted that if I ever wanted to pay cash to send a child through medical school, I could sell just one of those vases. I keep 'em up there with nothing in 'em these days. Sad." The grandfather clock chimed the half hour. "Well, let's move on."

Alice cleared her throat. "Andra. We've got to go."

I shut the door and tramped down the back stairs to the car. Popping the trunk, I grabbed a value-priced tub of water and hoisted it onto the bumper. "If you work the nozzle, I'll hold my CamelBak for you to fill it."

Alice pressed the white button on the jug while I tried to keep the pouch's opening underneath. Water trickled from the white spout, like a hose with a kink. Alice cradled the container and shook it. "What's the matter? Why isn't any water coming out?"

We fiddled with the nozzle to make sure it was open all the way. When that didn't work, we peered through the clear plastic sides to spot obstructions. After numerous adjustments, we pressed the button to re-start the

flow. Our collective machinations slowed it from a trickle to a drip.

"It's going to take ten minutes to fill at this rate," I fumed. "Is there something else we can do?"

We twisted the white cap on the other end of the unit. When nothing happened, we held either end and shook the container. I was ready to drop-kick the thing across the yard just as Alice clamped the sides with her elbows and squeezed. Water streamed into my CamelBak, a somewhat normal flow. "I can't believe we're two college graduates, and we can't figure out how to make this thing work." I laughed to mask a shudder along my insides.

What was I doing? My walk was nothing more than a mid-life lark to stave off failure.

I thought a lot about failure during my training. When my career evaporated, I barged into a local outdoor store and bought a $100 pair of Salomon sneakers on credit. I walked across bridges and wondered how to rebuild a consulting practice I didn't enjoy. On lonely marsh pathways, I cried when I considered new beginnings. I poured frustration and despair into legs and feet and told Michael movement was changing my outlook.

Until I awoke one morning with a sore ankle. A swollen foot.

"Did you twist your ankle on a walk, Andra?" Michael lay next to me in bed and massaged puffy skin.

"No. I don't remember doing anything to it. My ankle just looked like this when I woke up."

Michael picked up his phone. "I'm making you an appointment with Stephen."

Stephen Khouri. Our chiropractor. While he adjusted college sports teams, he also took mortal patients like me. I sat in his office and watched him work tanned fingers around my ankle.

"It's dislocated. How much did you say you're walking again?"

"I've got to walk 444 miles in thirty-four days."

"When?"

"Less than two months from now. I start March 1."

Stephen's mouth dropped open. "And you started training when?"

"A couple of weeks ago."

"How many miles are you doing at a time?"

I only knew it wasn't enough, but I pretended mental calculations. "Eight miles?"

He scratched the fuzz on his head. "Other than the ankle, you're in great shape, Andra. You're keeping up your yoga practice, and it shows. I want you to come in once a week, and I'll adjust it. Really, injuries like this are pretty common among my athletes."

"I'm not an athlete." I shifted my 150-pound body on his table and rested my arms on my forties paunch.

"You're walking fifteen miles a day for thirty-four days?"

I nodded.

"You're an athlete. Now, let's take a crack at that ankle."

I pressed my face into the table and breathed through bone grinding on bone. Nobody ever called me an athlete.

Except Dad.

My father made an effort to change my mind about my athletic abilities sometime in my sixteenth year. When Mom bought a badminton set, Dad was the only person I wanted to play. Our birdies didn't flutter. They zoomed back and forth across the net. I stood in the Southern twilight, scratching mosquito bites, oblivious to everything but the thrill of beating my father at a game that required true athletic skill.

I always thought badminton gifted me with some coordination, but maybe Dad helped me find what already existed within myself.

I blinked into the steamy Mississippi morning. Why was I thinking about badminton when I had a book to launch? Four hundred and forty-four miles to walk?

Because walking across three states in thirty-four days required another level of grit.

Several other levels.

Maybe an entire quarry.

I unfolded a map of the Natchez Trace Parkway. Its

twelve sections reached the windshield when I opened it flat. Air from the vent mimicked ripples in the landscape. A bold line of highway snaked north, with eastward turns south of Jackson and near the Alabama state line. Meriwether Lewis stared at me, near the fold at the top of the third section, acknowledging my pilgrimage to his grave. An average of three days per section.

Eternity yawned before me. At the beginning of any project, I always struggled to partition it into sections. I crumpled the map and threw it in the back seat. If I finished, would anybody care enough to read my novel?

"We're here." Alice steered us into a pull-off. We stared at two stone pillars bisected by a wooden sign.

Natchez Trace Parkway. Brown and yellow. Green and white.

The beginning of everything.

"Well." I gripped the armrest to combat dizziness. Blood bansheed through my ears. But when I looked at Alice, I smiled. One of those fake smiles, like Mom and I always used when we wanted to pretend everything was fine.

Because everything was fine.

Really.

I dragged my eyes back to the window. "If you just take a couple of pictures of me in front of that sign, I can get started."

Green eyes blurred with every heartbeat as I trudged to my first marker. Four hundred and forty-four miles was a long way to walk. Doubt gripped my insides, choked my ribcage, rebelled against air, but when I turned, I struck my usual pose: Mouth yawning open in a round O. Black pants. Gray shirt. Eyes wide. My toddler smile.

For most of my life, faces masked truth. In that instant, I wanted to take refuge in the car and drive home. Back to Michael. To failed nor-malcy. I didn't know what I would do with my life, but I couldn't imagine anyone reading my words or caring about my walk. I couldn't fathom making a wage from the written word. I could get a job at Starbucks and stop my nonsense, my draining of our household in a pursuit

of a stupid dream. I—

"I think these will work." Alice returned my phone.

For a second, I wavered between jumping and not jumping, between the first step and total flight. When I saw the trust on Alice's face, I stood a little taller, banished doubt and took my phone. "I'm sure they will, but just in case…..." I scrolled through them. "I guess I should post one, right? Let everybody know I've started?"

"Yeah." Alice waited while I played with my phone, fighting to see the world through screens when experience magnified layers. Cemented memories.

"Okay. This one. Done." My mouth its widest. Fingers splayed. Me at my silliest.

Silence engulfed me.

Without anything to hide behind, my eyes sizzled to life. "I can't believe I'm crying." I swiped tears as Alice pulled me close. With a hug, she whispered, "Most people would never take five weeks to just walk. Alone. Through scary, remote, even dangerous places. You're here. You're doing it. Don't wish it away. Promise me you'll savor it, okay?"

The ground blurred, a lens out-of-focus.

How many souls passed there in 10,000 years?

One of them whispered.

"Get moving, girl."

Not Without My Father

I WALK ALONE

Green Day

My feet pogoed along the pavement of the Natchez Trace, two victims of adrenalin and the craving to launch a novel and make history. After I posted my open-mouthed picture in front of the parkway sign, my phone lit up with words of encouragement from readers around the globe, stalwart people who cheered my writing. I hoped they would bolster me through all 444 miles, because as long as they were there, I couldn't quit without public humiliation. At the starting line, they didn't disappoint.

> You're a badass, Andra!

> Go, Andra! Go!

> You've GOT this!

Praise was always light to my inner moth. I bounded across the road and stuck to the white line on the opposite side, a continuous ribbon of paint that stretched to middle Tennessee. I knelt on the pebbly tarmac and snapped a picture. Perspective merged the line with infinity. I choked on audacity and burning rubber, not caring whether I applied enough sunblock on my fair hands. Before I could push myself to stand, an engine rattled toward me. Hot fumes stung my face and slithered up my nostrils. I rolled sideways onto grass as an extended cab pickup blasted

past and disappeared around a bend.

The driver never braked. I couldn't tell if he saw me.

"Sheesh, Andra. Remember, you're just a five-seven white woman in a hat. Walking. These people aren't expecting you." I spoke into early spring air. If I talked to myself and no one heard me, that meant I wasn't crazy.

Right?

I scrolled through my texts again.

With you all the way, Andra!

You're gonna kill this!

Can't wait to see you in Tennessee!

And one from my mother.

Be careful.

No surprise she chose those words for her only daughter. Always pushing boundaries, stepping over lines.

I leaned into the railing of a concrete bridge. Cars blitzed underneath me. Each speeding vehicle was a time I jumped too soon. My first, disastrous marriage. My initial choice of career. Even my own entrepreneurial efforts. For me, life had always been about having the guts to jump.

At forty-four, I needed a place to land. A soft spot. Not a splat of bone and blood on concrete.

"You've already jumped, Andra. For real. No point doing it again." The back of my head scraped against the guardrail, and I comprehended my first victory.

Milepost 1.

Angst forgotten, I skipped to the bend in the road and hoisted my foot

along a sliver of browned steel bolted into grass, posts that would mark every mile of my uphill trek to Nashville. As my iPhone recorded the moment, I whispered, "There. Only 443 to go."

Anthills volcanoed along the pavement edge, and the shoulder fell into a ditch. "I hope it'll be okay if I just walk in the road." I picked up my step and hugged the sloped pavement on the southbound side, confident I would see approaching cars.

Even though I never saw what was coming in Life.

Near milepost 2, a white truck stopped. A man's uniformed arm waved me to his open window. "Great. This is where I'm gonna be told I can't walk the Trace. Barely two miles in." I inched toward him, one conversation ringing in my ears.

Before I left for Mississippi, my husband Michael had just one request. "Call the authorities along the Trace, Andra, and let them know what you're doing."

I dug in along my side of our shared desk and looked into his blue eyes. "Why? One of them'll just tell me I can't, and I'll have to quit before I start."

"Just promise me you'll call the National Park Service before you leave. If you let them know, I'll be happy." His left hand fiddled with a pen, but his eyes held my gaze.

My husband. He straddled an impossible white line. Support my insane dreams? Or protect me? If something happened to me, everyone would blame him.

I forced my lips to say what he wanted to hear.

"Okay."

But I never made that call.

As I sidled up to a truck with the logo of the United States Government emblazoned on its door, I cursed myself. Michael was always, always right. Why didn't I call them? At least put my blasted walk on their radar?

"What're you doing?" A peach-fuzzed guy smiled. He couldn't have been older than twenty-five.

I relaxed into the cool metal of his door. "Walking to Nashville."

"Walking the whole Trace? Really?"

"Yeah."

He shifted his truck into park. The smile slid from his face. "Nobody does that."

"I'm doing it."

His fingers tapped along the dashboard. After a few beats, he turned to me. "Well, just be careful. Congress cut our patrols to nothing out here. I'm part of a skeleton maintenance crew. I'll send word up the line, let everybody know what you're doing."

"Thanks."

He started to roll up his window before throwing out a last "Good luck!"

A deadlocked Congress cut funding to non-essential government programs like the National Park Service. When I planned my walk of the Natchez Trace Parkway, I didn't know I'd face diminished ranger patrols, shuttered points-of-interest and barebones maintenance. I arrived thinking if I got in trouble, I could summon a ranger anywhere along the route. But with next-to-no government employees on the Trace, I was even more isolated.

As I huffed into my third mile, my feet tingled. I picked up speed into my first easy hill. At the top, I celebrated milepost 3 with a smashed can of Miller High Life, empty trash from someone else's party.

The sun blistered the brim of my hat. My cheeks burned after one hour of walking. Three miles. Ten degrees warmer. I shifted my backpack to let air nibble my sweaty shirt. "Making good time."

Like making good time negated discomfort.

When I was growing up, making time was Dad's catchphrase on long road trips. "Gotta make good time, Linda. Can't stop for nothing, not even to pee." I remembered pinching my crotch together to keep from soiling myself while Dad drove past exit after exit. When we got to our final destination, I could barely walk through bladder pain, but I still made it to a real bathroom. Ladies didn't pee on the ground.

Familiar heat fired through my loins, my first experience with discomfort on the Natchez Trace.

I jogged past milepost 4. Another slight incline. A tunnel through trees. To shift my attention from the mounting insistence of my abdomen, I snapped pictures. Of baby wildflowers, infant heads a first homage to spring. Of rocks, strewn across another bridge. Of moss, clinging to the white edge of a road sign.

Jackson 90.

Mileposts 5 through 7 blitzed through the blur of photography. I stopped once to sip water, hoping deprivation would help with my urgent bladder. In four miles, I hadn't seen a single vehicle.

I shuddered and pressed onward, certain my father would be proud of the time I was making. After all, I was already at milepost 8. Two hours and thirty minutes from the starting line. I squinted up an embankment.

Elizabeth Female Academy.

"I can't believe I'm already here."

The first stop on my Natchez Trace book tour, Elizabeth Female Academy boasted the title "First Female College in the United States." While I wasn't sure that was true, I knew John James Audubon taught there in 1822. I imagined the Frenchman, lecturing about birds to full-skirted, corseted girls.

A sidewalk snaked through trees. I hovered there, afraid of ghosts another visit might conjure. Undocumented souls were slathered across the Natchez Trace. Vehicular traffic masked spirits.

But when it was quiet, when the road was still, I heard them.

Famous. Obscure.

I always did.

When I was a toddler, voices clamored in my head. I imagined my pretend friends into being. Ossie and Palolah were the first. Adult features and mannerisms cloaked in tiny bodies.

About a year later, Steve joined my made-up melange. I modeled him after the boyfriend on the television show *Petticoat Junction*.

As I grew, my companions expanded and morphed. They waited in the wings when I played a tough character onstage. As my first marriage imploded, they dried my tears. For most of my life, they were stalwarts who never left me, and they didn't expect anything in return.

Until the economy crashed and failure chewed my

insides raw.

"You can tell our stories, you know." They forced me to name their words and taunted me to make their stories live against the backdrop of a timeless highway.

Elizabeth Female Academy was a clearing ringed by a broken fence. A lone brick wall cut through its heart. Two windows were eyeballs in a face, with a ragged hearth for a mouth. I stepped over the barrier.

Into forbidden territory.

I spread my lunch inside an empty window. As I ran my hands along rough brick, I wondered whether John James Audubon ever stood where I stood, touched what I touched.

Bladder pain twitched me back to the present. I had to go. Real toilet or not. I shrugged from my backpack and found my toilet paper. Around the corner, blank dirt beckoned me. Nothing grew in a foot-wide ring. The air was pungent with urine. I whipped my pants down and winced through the interminable stream.

Stiff legs carried me to the highway. At milepost 9, a car charged over the horizon and swerved toward me, a G for Georgia Bulldogs on its front bumper. I rocked foot-to-foot as the window bisected Dad's jowled face. "We just had the best fried chicken. I mean, it was amazing. Wasn't it, Alice?"

"Yep."

My stomach threatened to reject my lunch of peanut butter sandwich, almonds and a peanut protein bar. An overload of nuts. I licked salty lips and stretched my heels. "Did you bring me any fried chicken?"

"Naw, but the guy there, he sang to everybody. *I Can't Help Myself.* Remember that song? He even sang it to me!" "Sugar Pie," Dad's bass boomed from the crack in the window, "Honey Bunch, you know—"

My eyes teared as I stomped away from the car. I couldn't believe I had six more miles to walk, with my senses screaming for juicy fried bird. "I'm going on, Dad."

"You don't want to hear about the fried chicken?"

Annoyance fired behind my eyes. Dad wouldn't get

to me, not on my first day. "Nope."

"At the end, then. I can finish telling you about that fried chicken."

I wheeled on him, my finger thrusting inches from his face. "If you mention fried chicken one more time, Dad, I'm gonna choke you with it."

Dad thought he could poke my temper with a cattle prod. He always laughed when he got a reaction. "Okay, then. We're going on now."

Fury overcame foot pain. I ignored needles in joints. Hot spots along toes. I blitzed through mileposts 10 and 11, but by milepost 12, I limped. Heat singed along the sides of my feet. I eased down an embankment and sat in a concrete rain gutter. With one hand, I ate a protein bar. A crow cawed behind me, causing me to choke on another peanut. I gathered my things, stunned it was only my first day.

Beyond milepost 13, men clustered around a trailer parked on the shoulder. My heart gurgled with memories of reactions to my walk. "But what if somebody kidnaps you/rapes you/ties you up in a barn and leaves you for dead after torturing you? What will you do?"

As I approached, I held my place on the white line. Men with trailers were not rapists. Or kidnappers. Or torturers. They were just men who happened to have a trailer.

A horse whinnied, followed by a crash. One man struggled with the spooked animal, tied to the end of a lead, while three others coaxed it into the trailer. When I was alongside them, the horse reared. Muscles strained in unison, a gritty, groaning symphony I understood. I hobbled past its chords to milepost 14.

I put agonized feet aside and focused on the beauty of the Trace: The watercolor canvas of eroded Loess cliffs; the spirit inhabitants of 1,000-year-old Emerald Mound; the variations in the yellow stripe at the highway's crowned heart. I was lost in description when hoofbeats pounded behind me.

A runaway horse, nostrils flaring from the exhilaration of a gallop that wouldn't stop. It clattered toward me. Majestic. Masculine. A living piece of Trace history.

Was it real? Or part of the haunted scenery?

When I looked away, Dad's car idled across from milepost 15. "Did you see that horse?" I called to Alice.

"What horse?"

They were gone. The men. The horses. The trailer. All of it.

Was the Trace toying with me?

ONE VISION (FRIED CHICKEN)
Queen

I took Andra to get some of that heavenly fried chicken. Soon as she was done with her second day of walking, we rushed her on up to Lorman, Mississippi to that Old Country Store. Miles 15 to 30 was so hot, I thought she was gonna fall out before we made it. Place closed at 3pm. She finished at 2:40.

I told old Alice to punch it, and we squeaked in there at ten minutes to three. Clomped on up them rickety steps and headed straight in. When Andra saw the inside of that place, it was the happiest I'd seen her in two days. She wobbled along the main room with its dusty shelves of junk. One of them women had to help her to the buffet.

I tell you, though. Andra perked right up when she saw food. She smiled one of them smiles that's been lighting me up for the whole of her life, and she piled her plate high. Two pieces of fried chicken. Fluffy mashed potatoes. Green beans with ham swimming in 'em. Even took a couple of them barbecue ribs.

By the time she got to our table, that girl was healed. Her and Alice laughed about some frilly dress hanging in the back corner. Between mouthfuls, Andra said she might just buy it to wear on Mardi Gras.

"It's supposed to get cold tomorrow," I told her. "Winter storm coming through."

Andra chewed a double bite of meat. "Don't tell me that, Dad."

"Well, you gotta be prepared."

Alice looked from me to Andra. "I guess the dress could be another layer."

"Oh, I'll do it without the dress. Dad's right. It's supposed to be highs in the twenties on Mardi Gras."

"You gonna walk in that?" I crossed my arms and hoped not, but I knew my daughter.

She was a bulldog.

Like me.

She reached for a big slab of apple pie and vanilla ice cream. "I have to, Dad."

"Why?"

"Because I said I would."

I watched that girl of mine head to the back to pay. That old Mister D took her money and asked about her book. She handed him some cards, and he promised to keep 'em prominent, right next to the register. I hoped he wasn't getting her hopes up, with her wrecked feet and all.

Next breath, Mister D was singing.

I Can't Help Myself.

Only he done gone and changed the words. He pointed at me and sang, "You know that man loves you."

Andra looked back at me, and her face was all joyful, like she was having the time of her life.

I'VE BEEN EVERYWHERE

Johnny Cash

For two days, I followed Alice through Natchez mansions and ruins, and I stopped to tell strangers my stories while she snapped pictures of I-don't-know-what-all. I'll never understand them architects, even though my daughter done gone and married one.

I try to love him. And everything.

But when we checked out of Hope Farm and drove to our next stop, I didn't rightly know what to do. The place was nowhere, really. A main street about three blocks long and nothing else. When Alice and me got there, I took in the Victorian quality of the place. I refinished enough Victorian furniture to know the era when I see it, in spite of not being no architect.

When that owner-lady took us inside, I couldn't abide.

"No stairs. I cain't do stairs." I looked at Alice and tried not to be all pitiful. "You tell 'em."

She pushed them glasses up her nose and smiled at me. 'Cause I'm charming. "I'll check out the room, Roy. See what's what."

While that proprietor woman led her up them stairs, I poked around the vestibule. My fingers itched to refinish some empire mahogany even as they rubbed against an oak desk. Maybe I missed my calling, outfitting old homes for guests.

Alice interrupted my dreaming.

"We can't share that room, Roy. It's nice, but the bath-

room is open, and......um......"

I knew she didn't want to be exposed to the likes of me, peeing in the commode. But I'm charming, remember?

"That's all right." I shifted to that owner-lady. "What else you got? Something where me, Alice and my daughter can triple up?" I crossed my mental fingers and hoped I wouldn't have to pay for the upgrade.

Turns out, the owner-lady smiled. "Well. I might be able to get you into this place around the corner. It's a rental, but we know the owners. People just moved out. There's a bedroom, and maybe you can sleep on the couch?" She looked me up and down like she doubted my ability to bunk like I was in the Army.

I could tell her a few things about Army life.

Germany. 1953. The Black Forest. My feet froze inside fur-lined boots when I went on patrol. I smoked cigarettes to warm my insides, but I never let anyone snap my picture with one lit. They was always behind my ears, no matter what. Regardless of how cold I was, I had an image to preserve.

For posterity.

If I ever had posterity.

Right then, my posterity was wandering up the Natchez Trace, a place I'd barely heard of, all for the love of some book I hadn't read. I cleared my throat. "Ma'am. You a reader? Maybe I can interest you in this here book."

Alice pinched my arm. "Roy. Not now."

I set my feet to follow the owner-lady. Because I couldn't do stairs. Nope. They was too much for me at my age.

WALK
Foo Fighters

Winter storm Titan bowled across Mississippi in the early morning hours of my third day. I left Miss Ethel's for good and slogged through fifteen miles in sleet, frozen biscuits my only comfort. The cold ransacked my tendons and shredded my joints. I set out from milepost 30 barely able to walk. When I staggered up to milepost 45, tortured tears froze on my cheeks. I trained for two months and believed I was prepared. In three fifteen mile days, the Trace showed me who was master.

But Mardi Gras was the next day. How could it not be a party?

While Alice and Dad checked into our next place, I walked my daily fifteen. Without my guiding influence, Dad looked at Alice and proclaimed, "I can't do stairs. No more stairs. You tell 'em."

"But you just have to tell Dad he doesn't have a choice," I sputtered when she picked me up at milepost 45.

"I tried, Andra."

"He didn't have any problem doing the stairs at Miss Ethel's. He went up-and-down a hundred times to talk to her. He's just being lazy."

"Well, maybe he thought these stairs were steeper. Or something." Alice slowed to make a turn.

"This is the Natchez Trace. There's nothing out here. I got us into the only decent bed and breakfast for miles. I read the reviews online and couldn't wait to stay there."

"Well, the bed and breakfast owners were really helpful. They found us something else."

I looked at the main house, the real accommodation, the one I reserved. A pristine Victorian, its lamplit windows beckoned me. I imagined a world of comfort befitting a Natchez Trace hiker: soft sheets, a soaking tub, and consistent heat. I shelved my dreams of collapsing inside it. "Great. I try to put us in classy B and B's. What did Dad find? A redneck hell hole?"

"It isn't that bad. Plus, the B and B owners said we could spend as much time as we want over at the B and B."

I bit my tongue and stared at Dad's castle. A squat yellow building, the porch spangled with plastic furniture and astroturf.

"It's usually a rental, but everybody's gone out of their way to make Roy happy. They put a board under the sofa cushions to make it easier for him to stand up. The innkeepers at the B and B even offered to make a special dinner for Mardi Gras. I know it isn't great, but everyone's really trying."

"Well, I'm gonna have to tell him he can't pull this again."

"Just don't say anything. I'll go get you some dinner."

"Is there anyplace to eat here?" I opened the door and prepared to hurl myself on the ground and crawl up the driveway.

"McDonalds. Or Sonic."

My stomach cartwheeled like it might spew forth an alien.

"Neither."

"You have to eat, Andra."

"But that stuff's not even food."

"Don't be such a snob." She touched my hand. "I'll go to Sonic. Their milkshakes are decent. It'll lubricate your joints."

The door swam through tears. I was too tired to suck a milkshake through a straw. Gritting my teeth, I fell to the driveway and sat there,  stunned from exhaustion and pain. "Do you think anybody's reading my book to make up for how stupid this stunt is?"

Alice reached through the door and squeezed my fingers. "Whether people read your book or not, you're doing something amazing, Andra. Really. Stop worrying about that and just experience the Trace."

"But I never thought I'd have to walk ten miles in sleet. In Mississippi. In March. I worried about heat, and now I'm afraid you're going to find me inside a frozen pillar of ice."

"There's something in that, too. I know you can find it."

I massaged my shattered calves and almost retched. "You've got more faith in me than I do."

"Sometimes, all anyone needs is somebody to believe in them. Now, let me go and get our tasty fast food feast."

Cable news blasted through the door. Acres of shag carpeting led in every direction.

"Dad! Turn that down!" I coughed to combat fresh Roy smell.

Dad patted the sofa. "Gotta sleep right here, but that's okay. I cain't do stairs."

"You've got to do stairs, Dad." I crabbed my hands up a paneled corner and pulled myself to stand. "Why can't you ever be happy with my choices?"

Dad turned up the television in response.

"Okay. Fine. I'm going back to the B and B—my choice—to eat my dinner."

I limped toward twinkling stained glass and barricaded myself in the sitting room. Would the owners find tear-stained sofa cushions and think I left a ring of sweat?

Alice was right about the chocolate milkshake, though. I inhaled it like food nirvana.

But when I went to bed, I couldn't sleep. I thrashed around the mattress, leg cramps and technicolor dreams a shaken-and-stirred cocktail of vicious insomnia.

Suffocating sounds caused me to lurch upright. I battled a sneeze and strained my ears. Dad's usual cacophony of sleep apnea machine and self-scratching didn't emanate from the next room. He grunted. And he strained.

Was he having a stroke? Or a seizure?

I clung to the wall and pulled my body into the adjacent room. Dad gripped the edge of the sofa, his face a Joker-like grimace in weak light.

"You okay, Dad?" I didn't whisper. Without his hearing aids, he'd never hear me. "What's the matter?"

"Gotta go to the latrine." He rocked against the sofa. "And I cain't........ get.........up."

He seesawed his top-heavy body into stick legs, but his arms weren't strong enough to push the rest of him to stand. I fought back images of Dad chopping wood, of him playing basketball, of him working outside for ten hours in summer heat.

I went to him, a foreign creature ravaged by Time, and I braced my arms under his. Familiar musk drifted up my nose, the scent of the man who made me. "Here, Dad. Lean on me. I've got you."

He teetered to his feet in a push-and-pull that wrenched my leg muscles. When all two hundred sixty pounds of Dad was upright, he stumbled. Momentum pushed me across the room. I careened into the far wall and cried renewed tears as stiff muscles flew in unnatural directions.

"I hate being old." Dad stuttered, stifled a sob. Jokes and feigned optimism hid in the shadows, covered by a black drape.

"I'd rather have you however you are than the alternative, Dad." I crawled across the floor and reached out to him, but he slapped my hand.

His voice cut through darkness, fired with resentment. "I don't want to have a stroke. Be helpless. I wish I could go ahead and die. Just die. I'd rather die than be like this."

Some tears are cathartic. Others are cruel. I sucked in air.

At its cruelest, Life makes a little girl watch her daddy cry.

Fifteen miles a day helped me comprehend aging. Already, I saw how  the body gave out, slowed down, refused to cooperate with the mind's intentions.

Were my lowest agonies what Dad's life was like all the time? I crouched in the corner, stunned awake by realization. Eighteen months before, Dad survived a ruptured appendix, but his near-death experience didn't shock me from my obsession with my own floundering career. On the phone, I lectured him about physical therapy. Diet. The hours he spent in his recliner. When he was slow to stand, it was easier to attribute his lethargy to 'Watkins Laziness,' an aversion to all forms of exercise that bordered on the pathological. Obliviousness became a shield against the reality of Dad's decline.

I helped him untangle himself from the hose of his sleep machine. "Dad. You're okay. You're with me, and I wouldn't have anyone else right now. Nobody finds heavenly fried chicken like you do."

Dad swiped his brown eyes. "I wanted to be here, Andra. I'm just not sure I can do it."

"You can, Dad. I know you can. You're the strongest person I know. Come on. The bathroom's just there." I tugged his arm. "Everything's going to be all right."

"But what if you hadn't heard me, Andra?" He closed the door in my face, and I stood there, wondering whether he would emerge. Alive. Whole. Ready to tackle another day.

When I settled him into his sleeping quarters and crawled back into bed, his question morphed into a crushing list of possibilities.

A reality no child ever wants to face.

Not Without My Father

WHEN THE SAINTS GO MARCHING IN
Louis Armstrong

Mardi Gras dawned on March 4, and I awoke to a panicked message from my husband Michael, more #areyoucrazy than #yougogirl.

> Dear: The forecast is calling for ice patches on the roads today in southern Mississippi. I really think you should consider a rest day. I love you.

I looked at Alice. Her glasses slid down her nose with every blow into thin kleenex. "Where's Dad?"

"At the big house."

I glanced into the main room. His rumpled coverlet. A vacant sofa. After his nighttime bathroom scare, Dad was awake, showered, shaved and out the door before breakfast. No dregs of the man from the middle of the night.

"What's the temperature outside?"

"Twenty-two." Her voice rattled inside a drum. "On the way up to twenty-seven. I won't tell you the wind chill."

I grabbed my phone off the night table. Reader texts littered my screen.

> Watching the weather and thinking of you today!

> Cold? What cold? You've so got this, Andra.

I buried my phone in the sheets and winched onto my side. Bloody gouges littered my feet. If I poked anywhere, skin broke like gauze. Blood and puss oozed onto the bedspread. Barely 8 o'clock, and already my body groaned like I walked my daily fifteen.

I stared at the ceiling too early on a polar morning, and I wondered who was crazier. Dad, because he agreed to take a long car trip when he couldn't climb stairs, get up from a low chair or be apart from a toilet for ten minutes? Or me, for knowing I'd force myself to walk through a blizzard on a forgotten highway if it meant I might reclaim my life from the ashes of failure?

I couldn't rest on my fourth day. After three fifteen mile slogs, I comprehended how stupid my walk was. Twenty miles or more in one day was a chasm I couldn't imagine. Whatever the weather, I had to walk. An icy highway was a minor chord in a concerto of pain.

My legs refused to bend when my feet hit the floor, but I forced them to totter to my suitcase. I chewed four Advil and pulled out a navy sweatshirt with "Nashville" sewn across the front. Incentive and impossibility were woven through every thread. "I guess I'd better use extra layers."

Alice hovered in the doorway. "I really think maybe you should listen to Michael. You know, take a rest day." She pointed to my macerated pinky toes, victims of the crowning in the road. Crowning: The tilt in the pavement that allows water to run off. See also: The slope in tarmac that gnaws at feet and renders them chewed-up, tortured stumps. "Your feet are pretty bad. Maybe they'd be happier if you gave them a break."

I flinched as I forced a wool sock over carnage. It stuck to blister band-aids and duct tape ringed in puss. "I can't rest today, Alice."

"Why not?" She honked her nose into a tissue. "Nobody would blame you for taking a day off in weather like this."

"I can't take an unscheduled rest day during the first week of this walk. Meriwether Lewis wouldn't do that. It would be like........quitting.........almost."

She sat on the bed and turned me to face her. "You can make it up later. You're not making sense, Andra."

It didn't make sense, no matter how I construed it. At milepost 45, I crawled from the back seat and balled my gloved fingers to keep them warm. Taillights receded behind a scrim of sleet. It stuck to my lashes when I looked at the furious sky and whispered, "What about this is logical?"

I didn't have a single book event scheduled for the entire walk. My grand plan to garner media coverage was a bust. I was spending time with Dad, but I wasn't sure he could make it to the end. When I pulled out my iPhone to check the temperature, it was dead from cold.

I tightened my hood and leaned into sub-zero wind chill. Sleet crackled on the highway. Was it wrong for people to go for dreams in mid-life, to force my father into a journey he couldn't handle? I swung my arms and forced my legs to keep time, but activity only fueled memory. Of people who said no. Of folks who told me I'd probably be dead before anyone read anything I wrote. Of naysayers who preached the gospel of being happy with the life I had, because it was unseemly for a forty-four-year-old woman to try to be somebody. Of Dad's voice challenging me to succeed.

Did my walk shine a light on dreams unfulfilled, on paths not taken? I hoped to inspire others to take risks at any age. Yet, as I shivered across a bridge, I didn't know how to fuel anyone's dreams when I was already defeated.

"Stop feeling sorry for yourself, Andra. Lots of people are with you. Focus on them."

Music twittered in the background. Staggered beats built into a song. A convoy of motorcycles streamed over a hill to Tina Turner. *Rollin' on the River*. I ran my hand along a battered sign. *Little Bayou Pierre*, cracked white letters on a brown background. Nine o'clock on Mardi Gras, and all was well.

I waved beads of green and purple and gold, and I timed my footsteps to fading music. My shoes left footprints in an ice sheet along the roadway. If those motorcyclists could find something to celebrate during the winter that wouldn't die, so would I.

At milepost 48, my feet were senseless nubs, and my

hands froze inside my gloves. I eased my bottom onto the side of an overpass. With frozen muscles, it took precious seconds to sit. "I've got twelve more miles. On feet I can't feel. With hands that don't work." I blinked to keep my tears in check, lest they freeze my eyelids shut. I wedged a cold biscuit from my backpack and chewed a bite, friction that might work its way to my core.

"If dreams are rivers, I guess I'm just gonna roll."

Twenty minutes later, I huddled in the back seat of the Mercury. My whole body shuddered against the leather seat, and my fingers ached as warmth flowed from a thermos of hot tea. I spilled some when I tried to take a sip, scalding liquid I rubbed into my thigh. "What's the temperature? No. Wait. Don't tell me."

"It's twenty-six degrees," Dad crowed from the passenger seat. Every time I asked him if he was all right, he pretended not to hear me.

Alice glanced in the rear view mirror. "You've only been walking an hour, Andra. Maybe you should quit early today. We could try to find a king cake and celebrate Mardi Gras. You could even dress up for dinner tonight."

I shook my head and fanned steam into my face. "I'm at milepost 49. I've got to keep going. I told people I could do this, and I will."

"It's projected to get colder, and it's still sleeting." Alice looked at Dad for backup, but he gazed out the window.

I studied the winter glow outside. Blue tinge clung to everything, the frigid hue of icecaps. My fingers mapped the same eerie shade. Bruises crept into folds of skin and rendered my hands useless. I fumbled with my gloves and tugged them back on, a shield to hide the havoc the weather played on my body.

Dad tried to swivel in the front seat. "Heard the wind chill's not supposed to get out of the teens. I think you should call it a day, Andra."

"Is that because you aren't okay, Dad?"

"Me? Naw. I'm good. I'm just worried about you is all. And I think you should quit."

Before Alice could open her mouth and continue the two-on-one take-down, I guided my still-frozen fingers to the door latch. "Remember this morning? When we were on our way out here, Alice?"

"Yeah. It's colder now than it was then."

Why couldn't they understand? People who reached for impossible things didn't expect an easy walk in ideal weather. I slipped through my door and tapped on Alice's window. When she cracked it, I pounced. "The cold doesn't matter. We saw a blue heron in one of the bayous this morning. Remember?"

She pushed her glasses up the bridge of her nose and nodded. "But—"

"And you said—you said—seeing a blue heron at the beginning of my day was a sign of good luck. Who knows what seeing a blue heron at the beginning of Mardi Gras means, but I don't have time to look it up. I've just got to believe it's even more luck, one of this walk's joyous moments, because I've got eleven miles left to find joy in this day. If that bird can stand it out here, so can I."

I limped away from the car before I changed my mind. I didn't turn and wave when they drove in the other direction, lest I lose my resolve and summon them. Dad's receding taillights brought back another time he almost left me.

I was sixteen.

Dad flung a suitcase into the den. Its hard sides burst open, and wadded clothes rained to the floor. He tottered on his recliner, like if he rocked enough, it might catapult him through the door.

"I'm leaving you, Linda."

Mom stood by the kitchen sink, swabbing an invisible stain with a towel. "Oh, Roy. You are not."

I gripped the sofa, my head ping-ponging between them. Mom's towel squeaked through silence. Finally, Dad crumpled into his chair. "I can't do this anymore, Linda."

"What? What can't you do?" Mom's hands rubbed her anger into cabinet doors.

"This........this family stuff."

Tears welled in my teenage eyes. "Don't you love us, Dad?"

"I don't know, Andra. I don't know if I ever have."

"Roy!" Mom slapped her dishtowel against the edge of the counter and stomped over to him, hands on hips. "Don't you dare say that!"

He pushed past her and kneeled on the floor next to his things. One by one, he stuffed them in the suitcase and closed the brass clasps. "You gotta understand, Andra. All I do is work, work, work a job I can't stand to provide for this family. To provide for you. And I hate it. Every day of my life, I hate it."

Mom blocked Dad's path to the door. When he tried to push past her, they struggled. She kicked the suitcase and pounded his shoulders, each lash drawing a fresh sob from my mother. "Stop saying those things! Right now! You're not the only one who's giving more than they're getting!"

My parents blurred together in a tangle of arms and legs. When Dad pushed Mom away, she tripped and landed in a heap. She watched him with red-rimmed, animal eyes.

Dad's gaze dug a trench in the floor. Suitcase. Door. I plugged my ears against Mom's raging breath and covered my eyes to miss Dad's exit. If I didn't see him walk out, it wouldn't be true. Rapid heartbeats fired in my ears, counting out seconds. Ten. Twenty. My voice sliced through layers of tension.

"Where will you go, Daddy?"

"Don't know. I just........don't know."

"Can I call you?" Emotion ripped my core, the rending of my first heartbreak. "Maybe come see you sometime?"

He ran his hands through salt-and-pepper hair and studied the popcorn ceiling. "Dear God. How'd I wind up here?"

Shards of my heart ticked sixty seconds before he stepped over his suit-

case. He slumped down the hallway, toward my parents' bedroom. "Leave me be awhile, Linda," he whispered, right before he closed the door.

"Leave me be awhile." If I stuck to my walk, even when every part of me didn't want to, would I understand why Dad stayed to become an old man who was waiting to die?

Cold numbed memory. Or maybe focusing on the cold trumped thinking about the past. My lungs cracked with every inhale. I hobbled past mileposts 50 through 55 in a blur of frozen torment. With every step, my pinky toes ground into the sides of my shoes. Swollen more than twice their normal size, they refused to bend. Bone shoved into the ball of my foot with every step. Speed distributed the pain, but I couldn't maintain speed-walking pace for more than a few minutes before I had to stop, thaw my lungs and catch my breath. Rest, even for a few seconds, meant reconditioning my feet again.

When I hobbled around the curve, I gasped. *Rocky Springs.* Yellow lettering beckoned me into trees. I explored a path through a ghost town, an abandoned church the only reminder of the life that once bustled there. Trees clung to the sides of the trail, teeth protruding from gums. Their branches rained sleety dandruff.

I listened for notes tinkling through the wind. Garbled words I couldn't understand. Grunts of animals long-dead.

I forgot cold and pain in the joy of communing with the beauty of the Trace.

When I got out my phone and punched Alice's number, her voice warmed my ear. "Bring Dad to Rocky Springs. It's a couple more miles. He'll love the trees." I hung up and hurried to put some distance between us. Five more miles. To a shower. To a Mardi Gras feast. To warmth.

Did Dad ever find warmth after he almost left us that day? I strapped velcro tighter around my wrists to block the chill. When he emerged from the bedroom, he didn't have his suitcase. He walked through the house without looking at me. Mom stopped him at the door.

"Where are you going?"

"Nowhere, Linda. I'm going nowhere."

And he slipped outside. Mom held me while we listened to his truck's grinding start. Sound reversed down the driveway.

"Will he come back, Mom?"

Her sigh jangled against the side of my head. "He has to, Andra. He just has to."

"But that doesn't mean he will."

She peeled my arms from her waist and swayed toward their bedroom. Before she closed the door, she mumbled, "No. It doesn't."

ROAM IF YOU WANT TO

The B-52s

I seen a lot of things in my life.

When I was a younger man, I wanted to be somebody. I guess that's what everybody wants, ain't it?

But I watched my father farm the hard Tennessee land. I saw the toll it took on him. How it sent him out catting around every night of the week. First one bar and then another. Left my poor mother at home to wonder I-don't-know-what-all.

One of my first memories was of Dad acting ugly.

I couldn't have been more than two or three. A little scrap of a boy, I was. And Dad, he took me with him on his drinking jaunts. Let me entertain his friends on the bar while he got drunker and drunker.

'Course I enjoyed the attention. What kid don't like that kinda stuff?

What I didn't like was going home, Dad all fired up in his cups. Sometimes, I had to sit right next to him to make sure he kept that old truck in the road, and I could barely see over the dashboard.

One time, it was nigh on four in the morning when we got home. Dad couldn't even walk up the front steps, and all forty pounds of me couldn't drag him.

"Leave him be. Maybe he'll drown in his own puke and spare the rest of us."

My mother's voice rang out from the dark porch.

"*But Momma.*" *I groped my way to her, sitting in her favorite rocking chair, and put my head in her broad lap. "I don't want Dad to go nowhere. How will a boy like me learn to be a man without no daddy?"*

She took my chin in her hands. I could see some of that snuff she liked dribbling down the crease next to her mouth. Same lines I noticed when I looked in the mirror. And she told me her truth.

"*You learn to be a man, Son, by doing the opposite of everything that sorry drunk does. You grow up and be somebody, you hear me? Do good. Go to college. Get the hell out of this place. You marry a good woman, and you love her. Don't run around on her like your daddy does me.*"

"*What's Dad doing when he's running around on you?*"

She ruffled my cow-licked hair. "You'll figure it out. Soon enough. And if God gives you children, you be an example. Act right. Show them how to be good people, even when you don't feel like it. Don't you ever leave them stranded, without no daddy. You grow up to be the man your father ain't and make your momma proud of you."

I thought about that conversation with my mother, the day I almost left my family. Life didn't turn me into the somebody I dreamed of being, but even though my mother'd been gone since before Andra was born, I knew she'd be disappointed if I acted like my daddy. She was someplace.

And she would know.

WALK RIGHT BACK
The Everly Brothers

"I'm never, ever getting out," I muttered as I sank abused limbs and appendages into a jacuzzi tub. Salt water stung my lacerated feet. "Does all this pain mean infection?" I shouted over the jets. "I mean, what if one of my toes falls off?"

"Your toes aren't going to fall off, Andra." Alice banged around the bedroom. Packing. She was leaving the next day.

I would be alone. With Roy.

By milepost 75, I walked to Raymond, Mississippi, a suburb south of Jackson. Five days done. Twenty-nine to go. Repetitive motion consumed me. Most athletic shoes aren't made to absorb the shock of a foot striking tarmac five hours every day for a month. Even with gel inserts stacked three deep, over one million steps, taken the same way, will cause the walker unrelenting agony.

The surface of the roadbed made hot spots flare within minutes. The only compensation for road crowning was weaving all over and hoping for minimal consequences. When the wind blew in my face, I couldn't hear cars behind me, especially if they failed to lay on the horn.

Every night, I alternated soaking my feet with icing them. While that combination alleviated swelling, nothing kept blisters at bay. They formed between cracks in

my toes and down the sides of my feet. Puss bubbled along the edges of my toenails. I couldn't wait to lie in bed and let cold numb the torment.

"Where's Dad? He should've been back with ice by now."

Alice zipped her suitcase. "You know Roy. I'm sure he's up at the main house, spinning more stories."

We were at a new place, one with a real bed for Dad, sturdy new furniture and a jacuzzi. Every move gave Dad a new audience for his stories. I put my feet on the jets and imagined Dad up at the main house. In his pajamas, his impressive belly protruding through a wedge of unbuttoned shirt.

I didn't have to guess where he would start. On the Natchez Trace, he told the same story. Every time.

Dad was the only son of an alcoholic dairy farmer from East Tennessee. The fourth child of five. The longed-for boy after a string of girls. From the time Dad could walk, he accompanied my grandfather and his friends on their daily rounds. This speakeasy. That still. The other honky-tonk. All of them soused with booze, tobacco and women.

While my grandfather got drunk, my future father entertained everyone, his pudgy legs a whirl of interpretive dance along the sticky bar top. For tips of pennies, nickels and quarters, Dad smoked cigars at the age of two, and he filled his piggy bank with the change he earned from saying words like *damn*, *bitch*, and *fuck*. He was known around the county as Hot Shot, the toddler who smoked boxes of cigars, whose vocabulary streamed from a sewer.

I sloshed water and tried to envision my father as a child. A sleeveless sailor suit, his coy finger next to his lip. Honorable Mention splayed across his certificate for the National Children's Photography Contest. I conjured the only other photo I possessed from that era. A pudgy kid in front of a  bird bath, one-piece romper torn and bare knees filthy. His dirt-encrusted hand cradled a crude slingshot. Eyes burned through the yellowed frame, unsure whether to smile or hurl a rock at the viewfinder.

Whenever I remembered that look, I knew why they

called him Hot Shot.

And to a man called Hot Shot, doors existed to be opened.

"Dad! What are you doing? I'm naked in here!" I scrabbled for the shower curtain as Dad lumbered into the bathroom.

"Gotta go pee." He was already at the toilet, showering everything in range.

"Just please don't do anything else while I'm in here." I yanked the curtain closed and dunked my head underwater to obliterate the scene, to transport myself to another place. Somewhere peaceful. Quiet. Private.

To my five hours alone, walking the Trace.

I started my day at milepost 60. The air still nipped my fingers and chilled my face, but the sun won the battle with broken clouds.

My phone quieted to a few texts a day, leaving me with my hyperactive mind. My Natchez Trace walk was a unique way to launch a book, but it also kept me from what other writers with new books do: Check sales; despair; check sales; more despair; check sales; try to guilt everyone into buying book; check sales; hate everyone for not buying book; check sales; drink oneself into stupor; check sales; have drunken social media rant that ends with spouse seizing all electronic devices.

I didn't want to be that person, but I never realized giving myself five hours to walk through Nowhere would dredge up other things. How I still didn't know my father. Why I argued with my mother. I compartmentalized familial dysfunction with an effective streak of avoidance. When my mind wasn't occupied with texting and tweeting, why were my parents all I thought about?

On his western expedition, did Meriwether Lewis dwell on the unfathomable?

Less than a mile into my day, I gimped into a pull-off. *Lower Choctaw Boundary.* A sign mapped the old border of the Choctaw nation, with a star indicating where I stood. On the map of the Natchez Trace, the points of the star touched my starting point. An insurmountable line stretched northeast.

"This is why I shouldn't look at maps," I mumbled as I dragged my body onward through fifteen miles of cypress swamp. The road was a land bridge with no shoulder. Whenever a car sped toward me, I crawled down the embankment and waited until it passed. I remembered how often Dad's job as a forester required him to shoot snakes in swamps, and I tried to stay on the pavement, bounding between cars like Frogger in the old Atari video game.

Dad's flush whooshed me into the present. "I—"

"Dad! Get out!"

"I got your ice, Andra. Sorry if it's all melted. I got over there, and—"

"Got to talking. I know, Dad. It's okay."

I always told Dad it was okay even though he wasn't sorry.

Dad's rambling exits were at the heart of my childhood angst. I was asleep in the back seat by the time he finished talking to everyone in a place. Cowering in the car was better than being the last person to leave, because, to me, that meant everyone got so tired of listening to Dad talk, they cleared out to get away from him. I never could understand why Dad didn't notice glazed eyes or furtive looks or hidden signals for rescue. He just kept talking.

His unbroken stream of conversation continued as I eased myself into bed and propped an ice pack against one bulbous foot. "Got to get you to sign some books, Andra."

When he was in college, Dad worked for Southwestern of Nashville, selling Bibles door-to-door every summer. I teased him with the image of himself, young again, reliving his time in the trenches. We kept a stash of books in the trunk, and Dad used his Bible-selling tactics to hock a story about the ghost of Meriwether Lewis to every unsuspecting person he met.

Dad's buyers always wanted signed copies. As Dad charted out his next  sales day, he made sure he had the necessary tools to close the deal. Maybe that was how he got through three summers in college, selling books. His purpose was sales, and he was determined to do it right.

Even if that meant making me sign books when I was

annihilated.

"I'll do it tomorrow, Dad." I buried my head under a pillow, but Dad's finger tapped the other side.

"I can't sell them if they ain't signed."

I flung the pillow across the room. "I said tomorrow."

"People don't want to buy books if they ain't signed by the writer."

"Dad—"

"I really need you to sign them books." He stood at the foot of the bed, arms crossed above his stomach. Unmoving.

The ice pack crashed to the floor, and my eyes teared when my feet hit heart pine. "Dad, is it possible for you to be quiet for five minutes? Just five minutes?"

"But them books won't sign themselves, Andra."

I stomped toward the car. Torture bolted up my legs. Before I reached the door, Alice was through it. "I'll get the books, Andra. Lie back down."

Dad planted himself between me and the bed. "Got to sign them books. I can't sell them otherwise."

And I wondered where I got my obstinance.

In a couple of days, Dad went from unable to stand on his own to a whirlwind of activity. Watching him exhausted me.

I snatched a few from Alice's hands and carved my name into a page. "Dad. I could've done this in the morning. On the way to walk."

"You'd forget."

"I would not forget!!! How could I possibly forget when you won't cease your nagging until I sign freaking books???" I almost threw one at him, but instead, I piled them next to my night table. If I turned around, I would see the smile tugging the edges of Dad's lips, his satisfaction at getting to me. Push-pull. See-saw. It was the fulcrum of our relationship.

I took a deep breath and crawled back into bed. "Don't you forget them in the morning, Old Man."

"I won't." Dad tottered to the window and rooted around a grocery bag. "Where's my sugar-free cookies? I need to eat one before I go to bed."

I eyed Dad's distended gut. "You don't need another cookie, Dad."

"Your blood sugar was 171 this morning, Roy." Alice plopped onto the mattress. I bet she counted the seconds until she could drive away from our insanity. And all I wanted to do was kneel at her feet and plead, "Please don't leave me. Don't leave me alone with him. We'll kill each other."

"Them cookies are sugar-free. That means I can eat 'em." Dad rummaged through another plastic bag. Protein bars and cashews rained onto the floor.

I lurched toward the shambles. "Oh. My. God. Dad. Will you please go to bed?" By the time I crisscrossed my sore legs and started picking up spilled food, Dad was onto another bag. "Dad—"

"Roy!" Alice rattled a package. Dad leapt toward her. He tore into the wrapping and stuffed two cookies into his mouth. "Think I'll go to bed now," he crunched through the words. Once his door was closed, I prostrated myself at Alice's feet.

"Please don't leave me. I'm going to kill him. Please stay and save me from killing him."

"He's killing himself. With food."

I finished with the mess and strained to stand, my hands digging into the side of a wingback chair. "When did he become the child here? Because I'm a sorry parent."

Alice turned out the light. "Enjoy this time, Andra. Even this. You're gonna miss it when he's gone."

I whispered into darkness. "I'll never, ever miss this."

Would I?

WALK LIKE A MAN

The Four Seasons

"I'm gonna stick close to you today, Andra." Dad surveyed thick commuter traffic as it motored past milepost 90 outside Jackson, Mississippi. "They's a lot of cars here, so if you don't mind, I wanna keep you where I can see you."

I shrugged into my backpack and sighed. "I'll be fine, Dad…..but if it'll make you feel better…….."

He turned and eased himself into the driver's seat, his knuckles white as he gripped the door to compensate for legs that couldn't hold his weight. When the car tilted and he was settled, I handed him my phone. "Take my picture."

Dad studied the device like it might zap him with a thousand volt electrical current. "Don't know how to work these new-fangled phones."

Smartphones were another language to a man Dad's age. He retired before the advent of the desktop computer. I remembered visiting his office. Every surface was littered with paper. Maps. Charts. Lists. Remnants of trees he bought and sold.

I forced the contraption into his unwilling hands. "Just push this button. The gray one. Right here."

On the Trace, I started each day with my back to the car, my first milepost in the foreground. Unbeknownst to me, Alice took my picture as I staggered away every

morning. She asked me to maintain that tradition, and after everything she did during my first 90 miles, I wanted to honor her.

I had no idea how to walk away from a milepost and snap a backside selfie. Not without a mirror and the ego of a Kardashian.

I stumbled a few steps and turned back to the car. "Did you get it?"

"Don't know." Dad dangled my iPhone between two fingers, and I ran to the window to keep it from smashing on pavement. It was my only camera, and I still had 354 miles to go.

"Really, Dad. You don't need to follow me around all day." I glanced at the shot: His thumbprint, with me and most of the milepost blurred in the background. I sighed and stuffed the phone in my pocket. "I'll be okay."

"Well, that lady yesterday said you was in danger. The one that stopped. Remember her? Worked for the state or something. On her way to Vicksburg. There's some mean people around here. That's what she said." He drummed his fingers on the steering wheel. "Tell you what. I'll pull into them rest areas and sell books to the people that stop. When I see you coming, I'll go on to the next one."

"Whatever. Do whatever makes you happy, Dad. I'm gonna get started."

Frozen joints eased into the rhythm of walking. Puss stuck my toes together. At milepost 91, I stopped to snap a photo underneath a spring sky. Cornflower blue hovered above grassy farmland, cut by a line of highway. When I closed my eyes, I smelled the sweet aura of fresh-cut hay.

In the field to my right, a cat slinked through spikes of grass. I shielded my eyes with one hand and studied its proportions. "Huh. That's an awfully big house cat."

It eased behind a clump of brush. Like a submarine scope, its head scanned the horizon. When it caught me in its cross hairs, it stopped.

I realized what it was when we locked eyes, when I knew I was prey to a Mississippi bobcat.

I couldn't remember what to do when confronted by a predator. Break eye contact? Wave my arms to make myself bigger? Shout? I sneaked a look at my phone.

Plenty of signal. I waffled between calling Dad and catching up with him.

After a minute-long staring match with the bobcat, I broke contact and sussed out the terrain. "If I just keep to the road and walk at my normal pace—don't run, Andra—I can make those trees. They're just a few hundred feet from here."

But once I peeled shaking hands from milepost 91, I flailed in a morass of flawed logic. Open spaces on the Trace were like swimming an ocean. The harder I pushed, the farther the horizon drifted. I kicked my step to a jog. Once, I looked back.

And remembered the story about Meriwether Lewis being chased into the Missouri River by a grizzly. His rifle was empty when the bear came after him, and he was alone. He dove into the water and awaited the bear's inevitable attack. Something else caught the grizzly bear's eye, and it fled along the bank, leaving Lewis uneaten.

Did Lewis feel like I did? I longed to run, to climb a tree, to beam myself somewhere else, but my tattered feet were cemented in place. Terror paralyzed me.

The bobcat started a slow creep toward me. Relaxed. Like it tracked easy prey. I jerked my gaze to the road ahead. A football field. Maybe two to go. Without looking back, I sprinted through the highway's heart. I prayed for a car, any car, and braced myself for claws tearing into flesh, for fangs at my throat, for—

A squeal knifed the air.

I forgot the pain in my feet, the stiffness in my heels, the agony in my hips. Never a runner, I didn't stop until milepost 92. Dad's car materialized where I waited, doubled over and heaving. He inched off the highway and rocked himself from the driver's seat. "Sold two books back there. I'm a good salesman, ain't I?"

I swallowed bile, a grenade through my insides. I lurched forward, hands on knees.

"Ain't I, huh? A good salesman?"

Cough-cough-cough. "Yes, Dad!"

"Well, okay. Traffic's pretty bad up ahead. I'm gonna

pull up there to that curve and wait. Gotta make sure you're okay."

While Dad gyrated through the driver's door, I lurched along the shoulder. Why was Dad always so oblivious? To him, Life was the next stranger, laughing at his stories. Another piece of junk. Why couldn't he see how much I needed him to shine his fading light on me?

For the next mile, I banished Dad and focused on my surroundings. Cars and trucks barreled around Jackson, forcing me to uneven grass. I couldn't walk on the road.

"At least, that bobcat won't follow me into this." I talked above the growl of a truck. It hugged the white line two feet from me, its speed around fifty. Vibrations rattled my ribcage and reverberated between my teeth.

At milepost 93, I whipped out my phone and snapped another picture. "Fireball Whiskey. A big bottle this time."

I made a game of photographing things along the side of the road. Five hours of monotony captured in pictures. At the end of each day, I scrolled through them and remembered. The ethereal quality of light. Brushes of bird wings. The primordial stench of swamp water.

But by Jackson, my photographs developed a troubling theme. Beer bottles, crushed beer cans, empty mini bottles and Costco-sized liquor containers accounted for a third of the garbage I encountered. In one mile, I found fifteen remnants of booze.

Which meant one in every three drivers could be driving under the influence, inches from me.

I kicked the plastic bottle and diverted my thoughts to the need for a pit stop. Traffic was too heavy for me to pee near the road, a proficiency I honed during my week-long walk from Natchez. I could drop trow and have my pants up, usually without seeing a car. From my virgin pee-on-the-

ground foray at Elizabeth Female Academy, I progressed to a streetwalking whore who could do it anywhere.

Just past milepost 93, I hiked into an empty pull-off. *Osburn Stand.*

Stands were once hubs of the Trace. Pioneers could

find a meal and a bed to break up the long walk home. Only two stands remain on the Natchez Trace, crude testaments to the creature comforts of a vanished era. At the Meriwether Lewis site, the stand where he died was consumed by fire long ago. A solitary stone step marks the spot he entered and never left.

Osburn Stand consisted of a trash can. A brown information sign. A treeless parking lot. Still, history whispered in the wind. If I closed my eyes, I imagined a cluster of clapboard lodgings. A horse's whinny. Clinking glass and raucous laughter.

I dropped my backpack and carried my dwindling toilet paper behind the sign. The stench of urine hit me as soon as I walked around it. "I wonder whether budget cuts are causing this problem. If there were enough rangers, people wouldn't be able to pee here."

Public restrooms on the Natchez Trace Parkway were spaced for drivers, not walkers. Dad carried rolls of toilet paper in the back seat, ready to deploy wherever and whenever the urge hit him. I skittered next to trees and lurked behind signs, never knowing when a park ranger might drive by and cite me for public indecency.

At least, I always dropped my stained toilet paper in the trash.

Nine mileposts later, another wave of nausea flattened me. I gripped milepost 102 with both hands to steady myself. Eighteen wheelers were forbidden on the Trace, but lacking patrols allowed truckers an illegal shortcut between Jackson-area interstates. Wildness and danger were ingrained in the history of the Natchez Trace, but squeezed funding added peril the pioneers never imagined.

When a camper veered off the pavement, it pushed me down an embankment. I landed in a mound of fire ants. Engine oil and exhaust fumes clogged my lungs as I raked ants from my arms before they bit me. "I'm going to throw up," I muttered. "Please God, don't let me throw up."

Dad steered the car into the shoulder and waved me over. I hobbled to the passenger side.

"Some guy tried to buy this Mercury back at that

store."

I dry-heaved and fell into the seat beside him. When I grabbed a white napkin and swabbed my face, it came away black.

Still, Dad kept talking. To him, stories were always right.

Even when they weren't.

"A preacher. Said these Mercury Marquis were the best cars ever made. Offered me cash for it, but I told him Linda'd kill me if I sold her car." Dad poked my arm with one finger, a tick he used to be sure people were paying attention.

I was too obliterated to smack him. I sparred with words instead.

Just like he wanted.

"Mom's gonna buy a red convertible as soon as you're dead, Dad. I don't know why you think she's the one who loves this car so much." I scrubbed more grit off my face and swallowed Gatorade. "This traffic is really getting to me." I spat a mouthful of Gatorade, mouthwash for the fumes.

Dad finally looked at me. "Maybe you ought to quit for today, Andra. Them cars is too thick to cut with a sharp knife."

The landscape blurred. Taillights and pavement. Noise and heat. Dad acknowledged me, without a story to mask his concern. And I was unstrung. When I didn't know what to say, obliviousness worked for me, too.

I gripped the top of the car and dragged myself to stand. "Three more miles, Dad. I can do three more miles!"

Dad leaned across the front seat. Open-faced. No barriers. "People'll understand if you quit, Andra."

"No."

"You can cut a day short."

"No." I hurled the empty Gatorade bottle past his head and gritted my teeth through stretches. Whatever he said, I wasn't going to let a fifteen

mile stretch of highway beat me.

"Why're you doing this to yourself? Nobody really expects you to finish this."

"I expect me to finish, Dad."

"Why?"

I did squats and pretended to consider his question.

Because I thought I'd sell more books?

What a joke.

Whenever I logged onto the internet, I avoided reader reviews and sales statistics, because I didn't want the lack of both to frustrate me. I didn't want to read what readers said. If sales were still under triple digits, as I suspected, I would quit.

Ignorance was a feather bed in hell. Did Meriwether Lewis feel the same, when he stood at the cusp of the Bitterroot Mountains? He knew his expedition would fail to find a water route to the Pacific. Yet, he led his team onward.

He proceeded on because he didn't have a choice.

I did.

So, why was I still walking?

I swayed northeast and waved Dad around me. He blocked a line of impatient cars. Drivers honked and yelled for him to observe the speed limit. Vehicles whiplashed me from every direction, their bumpers and tail-lights and side mirrors inches from me. If I raised the wrong arm six inches, a speeding car would've made it a bloody stump.

I leaned over ten lanes of traffic on Interstate 55, my ears throbbing with engine surround-sound in my very own live-action IMAX movie, and I whispered, "I will not complain about the quiet. I will not whine when I'm alone. I will not wish away the silence or the sinkholes in my life. Not after today."

I ripped myself from the concrete barrier and marched forward. Blood seeped through my sneakers, evidence of another popped blister. I ground my teeth and kept my eyes on the sliver of brown metal ahead.

Milepost 104.

Dad slipped the car onto grass. "I think I sold that ranger a book back there. She said she'd order it online."

"That's great, Dad." I trudged past the car, deter-mined to reach the end.

"Less than a mile. I have less than a mile to go." I

chanted through cracked lips. Whenever I licked them, I tasted grease and dirt. "I can do it. I can do it. I can do it."

Old Trace. The sign wagged over the road, marking a deep gouge parallel to the highway. I stopped and closed my eyes, trying to imagine a black-and-white place. When the world was buffalo and forest. Limitless sky. Unencumbered breeze. I took a cleansing breath, and when I raised my lids, I found the parkway silent. No cars. No motorcycles. No RV's.

I was alone. For a few seconds, I wallowed in a cocoon of peace.

I wandered to a hilltop and glimpsed one taillight. "Dad!" I forgot about my pledge to enjoy moments alone and forced my tortured limbs to run. "He's at milepost 105. That's the end. Right there. Oh my God, I'm almost done with this day." I hobbled over the last few steps, yanked the car door wide and threw myself into the passenger seat. My backpack smacked my head into the dashboard. I dragged it off and flung it behind me. Stale engine noise still buzzed inside my head. "Why aren't we moving, Dad?" My voice was a husky, broken version of someone I used to know.

When Dad cleared his throat, he got my attention. His fingers squeezed the steering wheel, but his eyes were on me. "You amaze me, Andra. I never knew you was this tough." He started the car. "Yep. I never knew you was this tough."

I covered my face with one hand to feign rest, to keep my father from seeing tears, drawn from the dry well of his sincere praise.

I DROVE ALL NIGHT

Cindi Lauper

People beat themselves up over all kinds of things as they get older, until they realize there ain't no point.

I never thought I was a very good daddy, but look at the example I had: A drunk womanizer who treated my sweet mother like garbage. She stuck with him, though, no matter what. Where I come from, families stayed together.

Sometime in her teens, I told Andra how I failed my parents. How I tried to love my father, in spite of his flaws. How I wished I could see my mother one more time, just to tell her I loved her.

Teenage girls. I'll never understand 'em. She always shooed me away, even those times I was crying, because I saw my life slipping through the inches she grew, the choices she made, the person she was becoming. She couldn't understand I just wanted her to avoid the mistakes I made. Kids never get that. They hear lectures and roll their eyes.

But Andra was a strong girl, just like my mother. Mom stood up to a lifetime of misery. Raised five children who mostly turned out right. Nobody ever doted on me like she did. Even when I towered over her, I was her baby, her pride, her miracle.

As I watched my daughter struggle to breathe, all I saw was my mother, near the end of her life. I wanted to be both decent husband and loyal son, but when the chamber around my mother's heart filled up with fluid, I admit it. I

abandoned my wife. Left her in the kitchen of our rented place outside Nashville and raced across Tennessee.

I had to see my mother. Tell her I loved her one more time.

When I got there, she was drowning in that hospital bed. I fought with them doctors, told 'em to give her something—anything—to help her breathe, even as the hospital intercom paged me. A call from my wife, telling me she was leaving me and going home to her mother in Kentucky.

I stood in that sterile hallway, where I could almost see Death creeping in corners, and I wondered.

Who had to die?

If I left and went to my wife, would I miss the minute my mother was awake, when I could tell her how much I loved her?

If I stayed until the fluid squeezed my mother's lungs shut—and that could be weeks, according to them doctors—would I still have a wife?

I found my father, told him to sober up and sit a vigil by my mother's bedside. He owed her that, and for once, he didn't disagree. I stopped at the nurse's station and gave them folks a party-line phone number.

I crawled in my car.

And I drove all night.

To Eastern Kentucky.

My wife and I conceived our daughter in a downstairs bedroom. With the door open and her mother just across the hall.

I didn't know that, though.

When I got the call.

My strong, struggling daughter was barely more than an idea when I hotfooted it back to Tennessee.

My mother rasped her last breath.

But I didn't make it.

REDNECKS WHITE SOCKS AND BLUE RIBBON BEER
Johnny Russell

"Golly Molly, Andra! You almost hit that deer!"

"I saw it, Dad. I saw it!"

High beams couldn't slice through Mississippi murk. I struggled to navigate a narrow road void of glowing stripe or overhead light. Astronomy abandoned me.

"You sure this is the right way?"

"Yes, Dad!"

"How do you know?"

I streaked to a halt at a stop sign. My iPhone fought two bars of service to map our destination. Gibbes Store. Learned, Mississippi. "The Google Girl says it's just a couple more miles, Dad. This way."

Eyeballs glowed in dense forest. I imagined I drove through an episode of Scooby-Doo. The gang ran their psychedelic van through corridors spangled with creepy eyes. They always broke down. I punched the gas and hoped the Mercury was more dependable than a cartoon vehicle.

"I don't know why we had to drive to the backend of nowhere to eat."

"Best steaks around, Dad." As we rolled into town, I mumbled, "Dear God, I hope they're edible." But was it a town? A few ramshackle buildings and no street light meant anything in the Deep South. Fantasy led me to one conclusion: We drove through a wrinkle in Time and

found a living ghost town. My eyes swept the landscape. "There." I steered the car toward a wrecked building.

"That's the place? Looks like a dump to me."

I pulled in front and dropped him. "Oh, come on, Dad. You've lived in the South all your life. You ought to know better than anyone that dumps are the best places."

He grunted his way outside. "I'll check it out, Andra, but I ain't expecting much."

"Don't eat everything before I get in there!" I shouted into the crashing door.

Stardust highlighted an arm of the Milky Way as I climbed squeaky steps. Country music seeped through swinging front doors. When I opened one, I laughed at the tarnished brass *I shoot ammunition. Do you?* push plate. Shelves sagged around the periphery of a deep room, while plastic tables lined the middle.

Dad took up residence adjacent to a couple sipping red wine. "She put us right here. This 'un."

Before I assumed a seated position, I stared at Dad's broad back. "Hi. I'm Roy Watkins. From South Carolina," he crowed to the married couple who were probably enjoying a romantic date night, but Roy needed to meet strangers and share stories. I was determined to preempt him. "Dad! What are you having to eat?"

Dad's hands hovered over their food. "This is my daughter. Andra. She's walking the whole Natchez Trace, because she wrote this book. I got a card here, see? Book about Meriwether Lewis."

"Walking the Trace?" The woman smiled at me. "Nobody does that."

"Well, she is," Dad announced before I could respond. "She's walked all the way from Natchez. Got through Jackson today."

The lady dabbed her lips with a paper napkin. "All to launch a book? I hope the book's good enough to warrant the abuse."

"Don't know. Hadn't read it. Did I tell you it's about Meriwether Lewis?"

"Dad—"

"We got some paperbacks in the car."

"Dad—"

"If you buy one, she can sign it for you."

I yanked his sleeve and wedged myself between them, almost upending their wine. "I'm so sorry." I grabbed the bottle's neck before it crashed. "Dad gets carried away sometimes. Old age."

"I ain't too old to sell books. Used to spend my summers selling Bibles in—"

"Dad, the server's ready to take our order." I crumpled in my chair.

The woman moved closer and adjusted the angle of her chair. An unobstructed view of the Roy Show. I expected her to settle in for the next act, but instead she hoisted her purse into her lap and rummaged through it.

Maybe she was looking for a concealed weapon to shoot the vociferous old man who was ruining her date.

She pulled out a stuffed leather wallet. "I'd like to buy one of your books."

"You would?" Dad and I barked in unison.

"Of course." She unsnapped the clasp and fingered through bills. "If you were from around these parts, you'd know that John Grisham story."

Her husband chimed in. "Oh yeah. The one about the barn."

Dad punched my arm. "Go get her a book, Andra. And sign it."

"Wait a minute. I want to hear this story." I pulled my chair closer to her table.

"Well, when John Grisham wrote his first book—"

"Who's this John Grisham character?"

"Dad! He's a writer. Will you let her talk?" I thrust a plastic glass of unsweetened tea into his hands and hoped it would keep him occupied. "You're talking about *A Time to Kill*."

"*A Time to Kill*, yes."

"Ain't ever no time to kill."

"Dad!!!"

"All right. I'll be quiet."

I turned back to the woman. "Please. Go on."

"The book only came out in paperback, 'cause it was practically self-published. John bought a bunch and stored them in a friend's barn, where they sat. And sat. And sat. Until the roof leaked."

"Destroyed most of them," her husband interjected.

"Happened right before the movie *The Firm* came out. His books became real popular after that." She winked at me. "So I always buy paperbacks from undiscovered authors. Those Grisham paperbacks are worth tons. I've got several."

I floated from my chair, macerated feet forgotten. "I'll be right back."

As I stumbled into the starry night, Dad turned to the musicians and yelled, "You ever heard that song *Rednecks, White Socks and Blue Ribbon Beer?*"

I dug into the trunk and cradled my little green book. White letters glowed through starlight. Would our crazy father/daughter sales team ever become a story like the one I just heard? I couldn't imagine a hundred people reading my novel, let alone millions. I stood at the door and watched Dad, tapping his foot and singing along with the band.

"Rednecks, whiiiiiiiite socks and Blue Ribbon beer!"

Was Life about achieving success? Or was success a thing I made myself, following my rules? Whoever read my book, I was shocked to find myself having fun with Dad. People lit up when he talked and encouraged him to tell one more tale. I came back ready to hear him talk all night.

The final chords of Dad's song finished as I autographed my book and sat down to a two-inch slab of perfect pink medium rare-ness. Dad tucked into his piece of fish and talked through a bite. "I'm glad I insisted we come to this place."

"Did I hear you say you're from South Carolina?" The owner stood behind us, our plates reflected in her glasses.

"Yeah." Flecks of fish fell from Dad's mouth. "I live in Florence, and my daughter here's from Charleston."

"Ever heard of Denmark?"

For the second time in fifteen minutes, I almost

snapped my neck. "How do you know Denmark?"

"My only cousin lives there. She owns that antique store, the one in the old phone company building."

"You're Caroline's cousin?"

She nodded. "You know her?"

"She's my friend Alice's godmother. Alice just left this morning. She was my wingman all week, and she really wanted to come here, but you were closed last night."

"Oh my God. Alice Guess? I know her parents."

"I can't believe she just missed meeting you." I looked over at Dad, his chins mottled with remnants of dinner. "Can you believe that, Dad?"

"I been around long enough to believe just about anything, Andra. Just about anything."

YOU'LL NEVER WALK ALONE
Elvis Presley

I spent my first day of rest on my feet. As I shoved things into the car, I mourned the loss of the jacuzzi tub at our cozy inn. Dad stood beside his suitcase. Sugar-free cookies dangled from each hand.

"Aren't you gonna bring that bag out, Dad?"

"Can't bend over to pick it up. You get it."

"Why-oh-why-oh-why did Alice leave me?" Every muscle screeched when I rammed his suitcase into the back seat.

At the beginning of the trip, I mapped my rest days. Sleep until ten. A long, scalding bath. Carb-loaded lunch mid-afternoon, hand-delivered to my bedside. A nap followed by another bath. Lights out early.

Instead, I unloaded the car at a Marriott north of Jackson. While my legs wailed through dragging our things up three floors, Dad hung out in the lobby. Every time I stalked past, he responded to my murderous looks with, "I'm selling books!"

"I wish I could sell you," I muttered as I grabbed the last bit of groceries and slammed the trunk.

Dad teetered into our two-bedroom suite and crowed, "Now, this is a room! I got a sofa right in front of the TV and everything." He stepped around piles, rocked himself onto the sofa and started flipping channels.

"Dad! Can you at least tell me where—"

"Ssh. I'm watching this."

"Fox News? Seriously, Dad?"

He toggled the volume to STUN. Even with my bedroom door closed, I couldn't miss the developing story. A Malaysian jetliner bound for Beijing went missing shortly after takeoff from Kuala Lumpur. Dad morphed into his Gulf War I version. He spent hours worshipping the TV while talking heads speculated, ad-libbed and revealed secret military locations to fill air time.

Even with earplugs, sleep wouldn't come.

When I limped past Dad, he was too hypnotized by intrigue and hypothesis to notice the door crash. I stood in the hallway and tallied the cost of our remaining stops against the number of books we already sold. Desperate, I fantasized about buying my own room.

At another hotel.

But as I gimped to the elevator, sneakers in hand, I knew another room wasn't the answer. A couple hundred dollars in book sales would never cancel out the thousands I committed to the trip. Money bled from our savings for months, finite funds I feared I'd never recover. Expenses for sturdy outdoor wear and the right backpack. Supplies to train for an endurance walk. Publicity. Advertising. Free print copies for reviews. Every time I uttered the words 'Natchez Trace,' money evaporated.

I couldn't afford a pair of hiking sandals, but as I took in my decaying feet, I realized I didn't have a choice. Seven days of walking caused my toes to swell beyond the bounds of my sneakers. Every morning, I winced as I applied blister band-aids and layers of duct tape. Chunks of skin tore away each night. I expected raw bone to poke through remaining patches of flesh.

"At least, some open-toed Keens might give my abused toes a break. I'll just put them on my credit card." I maneuvered the car into traffic, determined to have something productive from failing to rest on a rest day.

I scraped my feet into every pair of hiking sandals in Jackson's paltry collection, but three stops later, I still didn't own new sandals. Salesperson after salesperson delivered the same news. "Too early in the season for those, but if you come back in a few weeks—"

"I don't have a few weeks." I fought to keep my voice light when I wanted to choke them with my smelly sock. "I'm walking the Trace, and—"

"The whole thing?"

"Uh-huh, and—"

"Well, no shoe's gonna cushion crazy."

I hobbled to the car, pounded the steering wheel and screamed. "Why can't freaking Meriwether Lewis be here to make me some blasted shoes?"

It was better than telling the salesperson to screw himself.

At my last stop, I settled on a clearance pair of Tevas with open toes. I tried not to notice red welts and oozing blisters in the floor mirror. "All this after seven days of walking."

"That's how you tore your feet up like that, just walking?"

I turned to find another salesperson standing next to me. His name tag read *Brad*.

"Yeah." I undid the velcro, determined not to talk about my Natchez Trace walk with another person who wouldn't care.

"Where're you walking?" He took the box and waited while I tried to pry my feet into sneakers. After watching me struggle for a few beats, he said, "You know. Maybe you should give me those things and wear these sandals out of here."

I whisked water from my eyes. Kindness. I forgot what it was in a slog of unkindness to self. Smiling, I traded shoes with him. "I'm walking the Trace."

"The Parkway?"

"Yeah."

"How far?"

"Natchez to Nashville."

"Wow. So you still got a ways to go, huh."

I tried to avoid nicking open skin with velcro and laughed. "Don't remind me."

"I've known some people who walked parts of it, but never the whole thing."

I stood and followed him to the register. "Well, now you know someone. Maybe. If I finish."

"Alternate sides of the highway every mile. It'll help with crowning." He put my old shoes in a bag and handed it to me. "Good luck. And be careful out there. Paltry ranger patrols between here and Tupelo. The feds don't give the Trace money for anything. Let us know if you make it to Nashville."

Why didn't I think of that strategy to deal with crowning? No wonder my left foot was pulpier than my right. I drove back to the hotel, stalked past Dad and fell asleep, convinced that sandals and my discovery would make my second week easier on my feet.

If I learned anything from my study of Meriwether Lewis, it should have been this: Ignorant assumptions about the unknown almost always heralded disaster.

HOLIDAY ROAD

Lindsey Buckingham

"Why am I crying?" The barren highway didn't answer.

It was the beginning of my second week. Fifteen miles past Jackson, the world was impenetrable forest with a strip of highway through its heart.

I wove past milepost 121. A Monday. Every step drilled into my toes. Tortured ankles and spent legs threatened to stop moving.

A familiar horn blasted behind me.

"Dad. Think about him, and he will appear."

He pulled onto the grass and motioned me over. His belly knocked the steering wheel. "I'm driving up to Vaiden. See that woman I grew up with. Eighty-nine years old, she is."

Needles thrummed along my left eye and pin cushioned an eyebrow. A migraine. I fought to focus on Dad.

"Everybody called me Hot Shot back then. 'That you, Hot Shot?' First thing she said when she picked up the phone."

I pretended understanding while my mind howled, "I will not give into this headache. I will not."

Wind lashed me into Dad's door. He leaned through the window. "I hope you didn't dent this Mercury. Linda'll kill you if you mess up her car."

"Dad—"

"Supposed to be gusts of up to thirty miles an hour

today, Andra. Coming from the north."

I tugged the stays of my hood taut. Fiery points of light cracked in the corner of one eye. "Damn," I whispered.

Dad put the car in gear. "I got to get going. See that woman. She called me Hot Shot, and—"

I hurled myself into the car and rained hormonal, time-of-the-month fury on him. "Why is it so freaking important to see someone you haven't laid eyes on since you were a kid?" I rubbed my left temple and heard my voice crack. "I know what's gonna happen. You're gonna drive over there, and get to reliving the good old days—"

"She called me Hot Shot. Did I tell you that?"

"Yes, Dad. Several times. And you're gonna get lost in your stories. And I'll be waiting by the side of the godforsaken road for hours." I blasted his face with morning breath. "Don't. You. Forget. I'll feel like those poor people, waiting for that lost Malaysian plane. Do you hear me? Don't you dare forget to pick me up."

"I won't." Dad closed the window, my signal to start my five hour walk through a wind tunnel.

With a migraine.

Physical pain dredged the well of painful memories.

"Toby Denham, your mother's here!" Second grade. Hot concrete dug into my tender legs when I scooted closer to the front of car line. Every time another car shot around the side of the building, I held my breath. Was that Mommy? Or Daddy? I took in the little girl next to me. Her wilted curls. Our teacher loomed over us, hands on hips. "What're we gonna do with you two?"

We were the only remaining kids.

The teacher glanced at her watch. "Well, I've got a pile of papers to grade before I head home. I'll give your parents a couple more minutes, but if they don't show, I'm gonna have to put you in daycare."

"No!" I squeaked, prostrate beneath her skirt's hem. "Please, please don't put me in daycare. I can clean your chalkboards, or dust your erasers, or—"

"Andra, that's silly." Her disdain knifed through me. "If you go to day-care, you can just play."

A car hurled into the parking lot, and the other little girl flashed a thumbs up. "Yessssss. That's my mom." She climbed into the front seat and smirked at me, but I focused on the ground. I wouldn't let her see angry tears. By the time my mother raced around the corner, I was in daycare, my mind a mishmash of insecure chanting.

How could my parents forget me?

When I could never, ever forget them?

Howling wind slapped my words into chafed cheeks. "You'd better not forget me, Hot Shot."

Near milepost 125, bullets of rain shot through me, a sideways down-pour that gained velocity with every gust. Niagara Falls streamed into my eyes. "Not this, too." I dug out migraine pills and dragged my sore gaze to the turbulence overhead. "I will not quit."

Rain mingled with tears as I swam an inland sea. Chilled liquid seeped through my rainproof clothing and doused my resolve. No matter how much I focused on the few feet I could see, I stumbled and fell in mud and weeds.

I rolled onto my back and pounded puddles with my fists. Beaten, I crawled toward the trees to wait out the storm. The sky above the Missis-sippi hills mutated. Purple to charcoal to gray. When I stood, a light mist clouded the air, and the world was still. Soggy earth sucked my hiking boots as I limped to the highway.

Another curse of the weather. I couldn't wear my just-purchased ath-letic sandals in the rain.

At milepost 133, a robin landed on the white line ahead of me. In good weather, birds swirled around me by the hundreds. Dappled grey and cardinal red. Magic music and feather kisses. When the breeze heralded a tweeted symphony, I stopped. Held my breath. And watched Nature preen.

When I noticed, Nature granted gifts that superseded

pain.

"What are you doing out here alone, little bird?" I followed it along the white line. "Are you hurt? Lost, maybe?"

But it didn't break its twiggy trajectory. It hopped a few steps and stopped. I froze when it turned and looked up at me.

"I wish I could read your mind."

I kept my step light, lest the vibration frighten the robin, and we walked together for a minute. Two minutes. The robin maintained its pattern of looking back every few seconds. Checking on me. Or, that's how I took it. Another magical gift from the Trace.

"Nobody will believe a robin walked with me," I breathed. At milepost 134, I fumbled with my pocket to retrieve my phone and snap enchantment. Before I touched it, the robin flew into the trees and rebuked me in a flutter of leaves.

We were making a memory.

Together.

Why couldn't I just experience it?

My senses were dulled by migraine drugs, drowned in a deluge and congealed by wind. I dragged out my phone anyway, to check the time. "One mile to go, and Hot Shot better be waiting for me." I blinked into another squall and kicked through the last steps of the day. When I walked up to the final milepost—135—Roy wasn't there.

My migraine dug out a hammer and pummeled the left side of my face. I clenched my teeth and called him. Once. Twice. Five times.

"Okay. This is just like when you were a kid, Andra. Distract yourself with something else until he gets here." I scanned the piney landscape. The closest pull-off was Robinson Road. Milepost 136.

One effing mile.

When I tried to take a few more steps to shorten the following day, my legs buckled. They were finished. Done. I crawled back to milepost 135 and pulled myself to my feet.

"Pictures. I can take pictures to pass the time." I

snapped several photos of my foot on the milepost. My feet adjacent to the milepost. My leg wrapped around the milepost.

Still no Dad.

I leaned against the milepost and worked the pictures in my photo app. Angle and light and contrast, visual relationships that mimicked connection in life.

Why did Dad and I always get the angles wrong?

I listened for anything that sounded engine-like, but the air carried birdsong. The applause of pine needles. Before my legs stiffened, I used the milepost to stretch my back, my hamstrings, my quads, my calves. One round of reps. Five rounds. Ten.

My voice mocked me as it pinged through trees. "Goddammit! Where is he?"

Fifteen minutes later, Dad's car wove into view. He rolled down his window, a chubby smile on his face, and threw open the passenger door. "I'm sorry, Andra. You know, I knocked on the door, and that woman opened it and a puff of smoke blew outta her mouth when she called me Hot Shot."

But I wasn't listening. Dad was never sorry when he said he was, and I never called him on it. Sorry was just a word he knew I expected. I stalked around the car and almost ripped his door off the hinge.

"Get out."

"Huh?" He was still smiling.

"Get. Out. I'm driving."

"You ain't gonna leave me here, are you?" Dad rocked his way to stand and looked at me.

"Don't tempt me," I shot back and climbed into the driver's seat, my temper a mask for childish tears I shed.

Forgotten.

Again.

Dad watched me from the passenger seat. The whole car listed to the right. My hands shook against the steering wheel. Sunglasses shielded emotion trapped behind

my eyes, wounded feelings streaked with red.

"You wouldn't believe that place. Vaiden, Mississippi. That woman had a farm—"

"I don't care, Dad."

"And it was the run down-est place I ever seen. Did I tell you she was eighty-nine?"

My knuckles were lobes of bone around tan leather. "Yes. You did. Several times."

"Well, she opened the door. 'Hello there, Hot Shot.' It was the first thing she said." Dad's laughter rocked the car, and I compensated by jerking the wheel left. He grabbed the dash and kept talking. "She called me Hot Shot, and—"

"Dad! You already said that!"

"Well, I know I did, Andra, but I just can't tell you how good it felt to be called Hot Shot after all these years."

"Just don't talk to me, Dad."

We motored along in silence, over ground I already covered. But I was with Hot Shot. He couldn't be quiet for long. If he was conscious, his mouth had to move.

"There's milepost 105...............104."

"Dad! I said don't talk."

"Okay...........103."

"Dad!!!!"

"Well, I don't understand why we got to backtrack so much. Why couldn't we stay closer to where you stopped today?"

"Why didn't you just stay with that woman in Vaiden, Mississippi?"

"She called me Hot Shot."

"Oh! My! God!!"

I screeched into the parking lot of the Jackson Marriott. Dad's hands scraped the dashboard. "What're you doing, trying to kill us all?"

I put the car in park and jumped out. Anger was my default position with my father. For ignoring me when I was growing up. For lecturing me through my teens. For always giving his attention to everyone but me. I whirled on him. "Why did you forget me? I told you you'd go over there and forget me." My chest shook against the bile that threatened to spew like hot lava.

Dad sat there. A little boy. Lost. "But she called me Hot Shot. She remembered me that way." His shoulders stooped as he climbed from the car and shuffled past me. "Probably the last time anybody in my life'll recall that part of who I am."

"Well, what about me, huh? I'm your daughter, and I'm still trying to figure out who you are!"

Dad ignored me and went inside. Light flickered when he fired up the television. By the time I turned off the car and hobbled inside, he was mesmerized, news screeching ever more preposterous speculation about the Malaysian plane.

I locked myself in the bathroom and tore off sweaty clothes. The vein above my left eye throbbed. While the tub filled with steaming water, I sat on the cold toilet and breathed in the scent of eucalyptus, bath salt I added to cleanse shredded feet. Water crashed, and I closed my eyes and pretended it was a waterfall.

When I turned off the faucet, Greta Van Sustern joined me in the bath. She barked a litany of guesses and innuendo at yet another assembled panel of experts. I dunked my head and held my breath until stars danced through darkness. Water sprayed everywhere when I surfaced and shouted, "Can you please turn that down, Dad?"

"Gotta find out what happened to that plane." Cable news swelled even louder as panelists engaged in a hackneyed crescendo of guessing games and speculative fiction. "I can't believe they don't know where it is."

"They'll never find that plane, Dad!!"

Just like I would never find my father. My dreams for connection swirled down the drain.

I bypassed sitting with him and slipped into my room. Foam earplugs blocked out another sensational non-news program. They muted Dad's diatribes, emo-

tional reactions to everything he saw and heard, designed to keep people watching. To foment controversy and discord. To divide viewers.

Some relationships are simple division.

I wrapped a pillow around my head. My mother was coming to relieve Dad of sole responsibility for me. Or to smother me. After two days together, Dad and I called her. Independently.

"Please come and save us from killing each other," we both pleaded in separate episodes.

She would spend three weeks on the Trace to finish the trip. If Dad was already driving me insane, I despaired at Mom's arrival. In the moment, I wanted her. But with distance and clarity?

Even though Dad was maddening, Mom and I clashed like feral cats fighting over the same turf. I wondered if we could kill each other with hurtful words, pointy things we wielded with vengeful precision. With expert calculation. With intimate knowledge of wounds to cause supreme pain. In recent months, we found a happier place. But our truce was too recent to hope it would last.

I smothered my head and mumbled, "I can't wait."

HAVE LOVE WILL TRAVEL
The Sonics

It ain't easy being caught between two women, especially if you love 'em.

My wife wanted a baby so bad. I kinda lost her after my daughter was born. She couldn't breastfeed. Didn't get no milk. But she wouldn't let no one else hold a bottle to feed Andra. Linda was the only one to change her, give her a bath, put her to bed.

I looked at the two of them sometimes, off in their own little womanly world, and I wondered....

What was the point of my being around?

Here I was, a man who'd been doted on by his mother and sisters, who was always the center of their worlds, even after they found husbands. A man who just buried his dear mother in the ground months before, and I was an outsider. An outcast. A third-wheel in his own home.

Linda was always protecting her children, never got tongue-tied. I used to watch her with Andra, and I had no idea how she did it. How does a fella find stuff to say to a little human being, day after day after day? I'd come home from work too tired to do anything more than chase Andra around the house in them Groucho Marx glasses. She shrieked and laughed and begged for more, but after five or ten minutes, I was done. I watched her, bobbing up and down between me and the TV in one of them dresses Linda liked so much, busting with stuff to tell me.

Only I didn't know how to listen.

When Linda called her, she always frittered away. Forgot about me. Left me stuck with my own ignorance about how to be a good dad.

She and Linda, they always talked about everything. They talked about the boys Andra chose to date. Never liked any of 'em, including that husband of hers. Andra used to call Linda every day once she got home from her first job. They'd talk for an hour or more, and I'd sit there, waiting for her to say she wanted to talk to me.

She never did. I was always the castaway.

But something changed around the time Andra turned thirty-three. Don't know what it was. All of a sudden, she was arguing with Linda all the time, them emotional, female fights I couldn't understand. They'd hurl insults and storm out of rooms and make each other cry and everything........I didn't know what to do.

Turns out, that's when Andra started calling me. A few minutes, at first, while Linda was at work. Conversations filled with gaps and stops and silences, but over the years, we worked it out. When Linda couldn't find the way back to Andra, I was the one who explained how to get there.

Because I finally saw my daughter as a woman, inside the little girl we made, and I knew how to talk to grown-ups. I entertained her with stories. Shared my Hot Shot routine. And somewhere in there, I gave her a nugget or two from inside, and hoped she knew what she meant to me.

FIELDS OF GOLD

Sting

Milepost 165.

A Thursday.

The Mississippi Hills were a Chinese army of pine trees, flanking me in every direction. Branches entwined like clasped fingers overhead, a canopy that blocked light. I directed Dad to French Camp. Milepost 180. Our next overnight stop.

"Check out the place, Dad. Maybe drag some of our stuff inside."

"Why? I can just wait for you."

"Because I might be in bed ten minutes faster if you get some stuff out of the car!"

"Does this place have a TV?"

"Goodbye, Dad."

I waved into his exhaust and prepared to muscle everything into another stop.

A vibration ran up my leg. I reached into my pocket and retrieved my phone. It worked overtime during my first week, flooded with messages of encouragement and support. But by the middle of week two, the torrent of upbeat sentences slowed to a trickle. My smartphone pierced the silence and frightened me when it beeped. The novelty of my walk wore off for everyone, about the time it steamrolled me.

Maybe they wouldn't notice if I quit.

My thumb ached as it scrolled over Alice's words.

Hey Andra.

Been thinking about you a lot this week.

Hope things are going okay.

Before I could stop myself, I typed three pathetic words.

I miss you.

I hit 'Send' and piled on a few more.

More than I can say.

Little dots pulsed in a comment bubble, mimicking Alice's brain thinking through a proper reply.

Is it that bad?

My data plan wasn't large enough to compose a comprehensive answer.

My father wasn't a nurturer. Not like Alice was. I stared into the chasm of remaining time before my mother landed in Mississippi. Emotion and exhaustion conjured a canyon so vast, so boundless I couldn't fathom the other side. On his watch, I took care of Dad, and I inherited my inability to nurture from him. Whatever misgivings I had about Mom melted in a haze of exhaustion and drained emotions. My knees buckled, and I collapsed, my shoulders shaking with sobs.

I couldn't type that I had to unload the car at our last bed and breakfast after a full fifteen mile day, because Dad couldn't believe he had to climb stairs again. I didn't know how to tell her I sent him for my dinner, and he was gone two hours. He ate a heaping plate of fried onion rings. And talked.

Always, he talked.

Even though he recounted his litany of food restrictions, he found a different place for dessert. I cringed when I imagined him chatting up the ice cream parlor staff. "I'm a diabetic, and I cain't eat sugar. And I'm on

Coumadin, so I cain't eat greens. And peanuts aggravate my hemorrhoids, so don't give me none of them.........But I'll take a triple dip of your butter pecan in a sugar cone."

When he finally returned with a squished bag of cold food, I couldn't find words to tell Alice I almost choked. I wouldn't admit I hauled everything to the car that morning. My tortured muscles forced it inside.

My spoiled thoughts were nothing compared to what Dad would likely tell Alice about quality time with me. The onslaught of my period was a siege in a lost war. My stomach was a putrid pulp. I was nauseated at one end, gassy at the other. With every movement, I complained, cried or cursed. I couldn't stand me.

Some adventure.

I picked myself up and brushed dirt and grass from my knees. Lies came easier when filtered through an electronic screen.

I'm all right.

Really.

Before I could change my mind, I hit 'Send,' stuffed my phone in my pocket and pressed onward. Technology and tantrums, two t's that always dwarfed my speed.

When I limped up to milepost 166 and tried to snap a shot of my foot, my stomach heaved. I leaned on the metal post and shrugged out of my backpack. "Where is my Natchez Trace Parkway map?" The sight of food made my stomach clench. Underneath my sandwich, I found the map and flipped through sections. "One-two. Three-four. Five! This is it." Lines and dots littered its surface.

"What's around here? Anything?" I wondered right before I doubled over. My bowels threatened to detonate, but the map showed nothing for ten miles. I wadded it up, zipped everything into my pack, pinched my legs together and forced them to walk. "If I just keep moving, I'll get past this," I whispered as I wiped cold sweat from my upper lip.

Ten steps, and my gut wrenched again. Holding my

butt cheeks together, I ran up an embankment. Into the woods. Without a care for snakes, bugs or poison ivy, I ripped down my pants, clutched a gum tree, and ejected a noxious pile of feces. I stepped away from the stench and tried to pick a splinter from my ass, but I couldn't turn my head far enough to see it. "This is what I get for lying to Alice. I should've just told her everything about this stupid trip sucks," I muttered as a car blasted its way south. "Dammit!" I jumped back and almost fell, my forgotten pants still around my ankles. Full-frontal, I faced the highway. The car blew its horn, leaving cackles of laughter and a rebel yell in its wake.

"Asshole!" I shouted, as another cramp sent me straddling the tree again. Explosive diarrhea shook my whole body. When I was finally done, I fumbled with my backpack to pull my toilet paper from the front pouch. Plastic broke free, and I stared at a zip-lock bag and sobbed. "Two squares of toilet paper. I can't clean all this with only two squares." I dumped everything on the ground, but my pack contained nothing wipe-worthy. Brown liquid ran down my fingers and puddled in my sleeves as I tried to mop up with two squares. I unscrewed the cap on a bottle of Gatorade, leaned over and launched the sticky drink between the folds of my butt crack. I used more to wash the mess from my legs and feet. When I pulled up my compression leggings, skin, sugar and shit squished under a layer of lycra.

"I quit! I quit! I quit!" Waves of pain shot through my legs as I ran down the grassy embankment, pounded my backpack on pavement and screamed. I whipped out my mobile phone to summon my father, to tell him I wasn't an adventurer, to come get me, to take me home, to embrace the failure I was. NO SERVICE taunted me from the upper left-hand corner of the screen.

"Dammit!" I slung my abused pack into tarmac a final time and sunk to my knees. "I can't even succeed at failing."

Three hundred and sixty degrees of trees, with a narrow road in between. I panned my eyes over the landscape until, seasick, I collapsed on a faded yellow dash of paint that marked the highway's center.

Maybe somebody would come along and run over

me. Put this torture session to an end. Maybe then I'd be a martyr to the memory of whoever, instead of a failed, feces-encrusted quitter.

Ten minutes later, when my darkest thoughts didn't summon a single vehicle, I zipped my phone into my pants and staggered on. Meriwether Lewis wouldn't quit, I told myself. Not when so many people were watching.

Who was I kidding? 'So many people' wasn't even fifty.

A flock of cardinals fluttered across the road ahead of me. A whirling red cloud. I dried tears with stained fingers and listened to their music ping-pong across pavement.

All my life, I believed cardinals were good luck. Mamaw, my mother's mother, collected cardinal paraphernalia and scattered splashes of red all over her house.

After Mamaw died, I believed every cardinal was a message from her. That she was somewhere, even if she was only in my heart. Or in a dancing pack of cardinals, leading me north.

Sunlight freckled the forest interior. I squinted through pine needles and barren branches for glimpses of red and gray. Color dove in time with the cardinal concerto. I tried for my camera, to capture the moment's mythic quality, but a feathered body buzzed my head. Fleeing wings whispered an order through a faint zephyr. "These moments are building blocks of memory.............live them. All of them."

Life was easier when I lived it once removed, but my walk was a baptism of moments. I drowned in experiences that pulled me under, slowed me down. I couldn't fathom how people like Meriwether Lewis ventured into the unknown, discovered new peoples, and propelled themselves onward by the force of determination. I was ready to quit over one upset stomach and shredded feet. How did Lewis and his men battle the elements for more than two years?

Cardinals flew through my sightline as I shifted my gaze northward. "There's some sunlight up ahead. If it isn't a mirage. Maybe I can get warm."

Forest gave way to a muddy field. Still dormant. Per-

colating with the rebirth of spring. Without realizing it, I ran. Earth licked my shoes as I galloped through a ditch. My lungs burned by the time I pulled up at the far end of the field and surveyed the landscape.

Green shoots, mottled with a thousand yellow heads. Daffodils nodded and swayed. I heard them whisper, "Stay here. With us."

When I threw off my backpack and collapsed in their midst, they clapped and welcomed me. I lay there, panting, while clouds merged and parted in the sky. I worked my arms through golden trumpets and ran stems between my fingers.

For the first time, I forgot my schedule. The next milepost. Where I needed to be.

Because I was where I needed to be.

In that field. Experiencing those moments. Without thinking about foot pain or a migraine. How much I stank. The reality of walking would be there when I decided to leave. Tears stung my eyes, and I swiped the grimy track one made to my hairline.

Images of Dad shimmered a few feet from me. Too preoccupied to talk to me when he got home from work. Too harried to sit through a family meal. Too tired to stay awake and watch television with me.

Or maybe he just never knew what to say. Awkwardness was often labeled something else by the human need to classify.

"Life gives us these intervals, these incredible gifts," I whispered into the sparkling air. "Why am I always too busy, too stressed, too overwhelmed to see them? Just like Dad always was when I was growing up?" I turned my head to gaze into a daffodil's eyeball. "This walk is supposed to be about these experiences. Right here. The magic and the mystery and the beauty that color the lines of our one brief and shining life."

When I adjusted my backpack and left that field, I stood at a junc-

tion. I looked south at a path of hardship and pain, and I raised my hand in a faint wave. "I'm leaving you now. This is the dividing line. You can't follow me. I've been given these joyous moments, and I'm going to focus on them."

I turned my face northward and took a few steps. Still agonizing, every one of them. But when a cardinal flew over my shoulder, its wings fluttered a message. "Your walk—and your life—will be different. I know it."

I heard my Mamaw's voice.

WALKING ON BROKEN GLASS

Annie Lennox

"You okay, Andra?" Dad waddled through the parking lot of Cole Creek Swamp. Milepost 176.

"I wouldn't get too close to me, Dad." I sat cross-legged on a wooden platform built between swirling-skirted cypress trees. Swamp water lapped against the dock, and peanut butter stuck my cheeks together. "Had a little accident a few miles back. Ran out of toilet paper."

"I got some if you—"

"No-no. I'm only four miles from the end. I'll just get to French Camp and shower."

"They got some good Mississippi mud pie at that place." He took a few steps toward me. "Want me to go get you a piece?"

"Sure. That'd be great." I leaned against rippled bark and wondered what lurked beneath black water. Was it a key ingredient in Mississippi mud? The sound of the car faded, and I was left with fish chasing the sun.

When did Dad and I switch places?

He was the child, weaving stories through carefree days, while I was the parent, reaching for panicked dreams, a middle-aged gasp to force life's math to tally.

And I was always dyslexic with math.

When I was in elementary school, Dad spent hours on the phone every night, a victim of the whims of

weather. Juggling the wood supply for his plant informed almost every evening of my childhood. I combed Barbie's hair and pretended not to hear him beg and bargain, curse and plead.

"You're going to turn around, Roy, and your daughter will be grown, and you won't have even talked to her." My mom whispered unwelcome advice in their bed when she thought I was asleep. She repeated it in my presence as she stood over his recliner with ice cream. She shouted it for the neighbors while she packed me into the car for another piano recital he failed to attend.

When he finally initiated a conversation of depth, it wasn't to say he was sorry. "I didn't tell my parents I loved them enough, Andra, and now I can't. If I could have just one minute with them today, I'd tell them I loved them one more time." He paused and rubbed his eyes. My bed rocked with his departing shot. "I don't think you love me."

At thirteen, I didn't comprehend Dad's meaning. I only heard surface words and phrases, sentiments akin to swamp water. In my hormone-rattled mind, he was just lecturing me.

I dragged one foot along the white line. Milepost 178. My hand slid from metal. I turned my thoughts to daffodils.

Joy. I discovered it one hour ago.

When I looked to my right, Dad was there.

"Dad......"

I slid toward him.

And I saw a car plow through me.

What did it feel like when the soul was knocked from the body? I went numb and threw my arms around my head. Through my elbows, I glimpsed two halves of a Mercedes. While I hovered between life and death, the pieces joined together and formed one unit that fled up the

 highway. It vaulted around a curve and disappeared.

Was this what Meriwether Lewis experienced when he died? Explosive light and seeping cold and paralysis? Could he really see the landscape around him after he was gone, as I wrote in my book?

Was my death some cosmic repayment for writing about him in the first place?

I braced myself for waves of pain. Broken limbs. Exposed bone and viscera.

But my feet were glued to white paint. I was still upright. Unscathed. Dad's car idled a few feet from me. When I looked at him, he smiled.

"I got your pie."

I rattled my head between my hands.

How did that happen?

The car never braked, but I was convinced it hit me. Angry molecules spun inside me, emotions I thought I scraped off and left in a daffodil field.

I leapt across the road and assaulted Dad. "You can't just stop in the middle of a highway to talk to me, Dad!"

"But I got your pie. Don't you want it?"

"Did you even see that car? It almost hit me." I rubbed my face with shaking hands. "I don't know how it didn't hit me. I'm sure it hit me. I know it did." Pebbled tar and yellow paint wobbled beneath me. Dead. I should be dead.

"What do you want me to do with this pie?"

I pounded the car with my fists. "You can take that pie and—"

Dad shrunk in his seat. Confusion lit up the lines on his face. How did he miss the almost-death of his daughter, her mangled body parts strewn over a federal parkway?

Or was I the problem? Maybe hallucinations were a logical part of a migrained-stomach-bugged-dehydrated-muscle-pained-shit-perfumed day.

Meanwhile, Dad's world was all about pie. Pie made him happy. Bringing me pie was a nurturing act, right? For the first time on the hellacious trip, Dad volunteered to do something for me. So what if it was a thing I didn't want, calories that wouldn't make my feet stop bleeding.

Inside my head, a voice screamed, "He's trying to connect, to take care of you, you stupid idiot." A cardinal

flew over the car's hood, a daffodil in its beak.

"Dad." I touched his shoulder. "Don't stop in the road and talk to me anymore, okay? It isn't safe. Somebody might rear end you, and I'd feel terrible if you got hurt."

"Well, back there you looked like you could use some pie."

"Bethel Mission is just ahead. Pull in there and wait for me, and I'll come and eat that pie."

"All right." He started to roll up his window.

"And don't eat it before I get there."

Laughter filtered through glass. "Don't worry, Andra. I already had mine."

I was full of Mississippi mud by the time I reached milepost 180. Two miles from the end, I sat within the faded lines of Bethel Mission and savored every gooey bite. Richness landed in my stomach like rocks, but I scraped the container clean.

And I wondered how I could walk fifteen miles a day and not lose a pound.

Dad picked me up and drove into the village of French Camp. One of the oldest settlements on the Trace, it was still an outpost in Mississippi wilderness. People came to gaze at the stars, to meditate with the Bible. We bounced down a dirt road to our cabin. A full kitchen and a bathroom I didn't have to share. Dad followed me inside.

"Not more stairs." He regarded a sketchy staircase along one wall. "You sure those things'll hold me? Maybe I'll sleep down here."

I lugged a box of food laden with enough sugar-free snacks to feed the tiny village of French Camp for a week. The table groaned when I slid stuff on top, but I was too tired to care if it buckled. "Just be comfortable, Dad. I'm going upstairs to bed."

It was our last night alone before my mother arrived. I surveyed my sloped room under the eaves and limped toward the bed, but I misjudged the angle of the ceiling and banged my head. A rough knot met my fingers along my hairline. What the hell was I thinking? In two weeks, we sold thirty books. I had a grand total of one event booked. A lone newspaper interview. In the history of marketing, it was the worst campaign ever launched.

"But the bed is comfortable," I mumbled as sank into the mattress. I covered my ears with a pillow to mask the blaring media speculation from the television downstairs, yet another sensational update on the missing Malaysian airliner. "God, I hope they find those people."

I couldn't remember closing my eyes.

Did I dream Dad's pronouncement? "I think when Linda comes, I'm gonna go home. Yep. That's what I'm gonna do."

I sat up on the bed and cringed. The window was a black square, a dusting of stars in one corner.

I shifted sore feet to the floor and forced them to carry my weight. I walked like C3PO, the droid from Star Wars. Five daily hours of walking transformed me into a robot.

As I felt my way toward the door, Dad's words drifted up the stairs.

"Yep. Think I'm gonna leave Linda to deal with this."

I pushed myself through the door and crashed downstairs. "What did you say?" I planted my body in front of the television and shouted over the reverberation. Dad shrunk in his cushioned chair and wouldn't look at me. Instead, he picked at the plaid fabric and mumbled. I stepped over his feet and sprayed sleep breath in his face. "Would you really leave me?"

I made my peace with the trek that afternoon, survived a brush with a speeding car, even thwarted an argument. Why did he always push me harder? Remind me not to be a failure? And reiterate that no matter how much broken glass I crunched with bloody feet, it would never, ever be enough to please him?

"Don't leave me now, Dad. Doing this with you, right now, at this moment in our lives—it should've been my dream all along. I don't care about this book anymore. I just want to spend time with you. With Mom, when she gets here. Don't take this experience away from me. From us. Please."

"But I almost got you killed today, Andra." His hefty

fingers prodded the remote. "I don't think I'm helping you any."

I touched the back of his splotched hand. "You got me a sandwich earlier, right? 'Best one on the Trace,' somebody said. And don't forget the pie. And all the books you're selling. How many is it now?"

"Most ever in one day, just today. Think I sold close to ten." He sat taller.

"There. See? I need you, Dad. And, more than that, I want to do this with you. Even when it's hard."

"But you're so much tougher than me, Andra." He shifted and tried to look around me. "I don't know how you do this, day after day after day."

"How do we do life day after day after day, Dad?"

"One step at a time, I reckon."

"That's right. And that's how we'll finish this trip: one glorious step at a time..........or, we'll kill each other."

Dad laughed with me. "Yeah. Probably kill each other. I guess we'll see."

"So you'll stay?"

"Let Linda get here. I'll decide in the morning. I got to get some sleep." He clicked the remote and shuffled to the stairs. At the bannister, he stopped. "Think they'll find those people? On that plane?"

"I hope so, Dad."

"Yeah. Me too."

WALK ON BY

Dionne Warwick

I wanted to go home because I was afraid.

There.

I said it.

I was afraid of what Linda's coming would do to my time with Andra. How I'd be outside their shorthand. Ringmaster for their arguments.

For almost ten years, I told Linda, "Andra's an adult, and you need to let her live her life. It's her knitting, the choices she makes."

But Linda, that woman is the stubbornest human being I ever laid eyes on. I don't even recall when it started, but she kept at Andra. Questioning her. Telling her what to do, and her a grown woman with a life of her own. Being betwixt them two was like standing in the worst part of a hurricane.

Something shifted, though. About the time Linda read Andra's book.

I found her in Andra's old bedroom. Crying and clutching that story.

"Is it that bad?" I asked her. 'Cause I ain't read the thing. I don't need to read a book to sell it.

She never answered me, but she got up off that bed, and she started calling her sisters, and before I knew it they all read Andra's book. They spent hours on the phone talking about I-don't-know-what-all, while I turned down my hearing aids and concentrated on the ballgame.

And she and Andra wasn't arguing so much anymore.

Lots of stuff gets past me, but I saw a change. They wasn't so strained and mad all the time.

And that's why I was afraid, on the eve of my wife's coming to Mississippi. I had time with Andra, all by myself. I didn't want to share it, to go back to farting around for the right words to say. I just wanted it to be me, and Andra, and selling them books.

For a little while longer.

Was that too much to ask?

I CAN TELL THAT WE ARE GONNA BE FRIENDS
The White Stripes

My second rest day dawned with Dad banging on my bedroom door at 8am. "We got to go see that Doc Jones. South of Tupelo."

I settled into Michael. He made the long trek to bring my mother from South Carolina to Mississippi. I tried to ignore Dad and let Michael rub my shoulder. "Maybe if we don't answer, he'll go away," Michael whispered.

"Hey. Hey, Andra!"

I sat up and sighed. "Do you really think he's gonna let us ignore him?"

The door knob rattled. "Hey! You awake? We got to go see Doc Jones today!"

For ten seconds, I held onto the rest day of my dreams: Snuggling with Michael until check-out; walking outside to find the car loaded and ready; hearing Michael say he didn't have to leave; driving straight to Bridges Hall Manor, our next stop; soaking in the tub while everyone else unloaded the car; and eating dinner in bed before passing out on my husband's chest.

Wood popped when Dad leaned his weight into the door, the insistent sound of reality. "We got to go, Andra. Doc Jones is expecting us. I done told him we was coming!"

Michael brushed a wisp of hair from my cheek and held me. "We'll be out in five minutes, Roy."

"Huh? I done told Doc—"

"He said five minutes, Dad!"

I clung to Michael to keep my pleas inside. I didn't think I could walk fifteen miles a day and spend three weeks with my parents. I was the world's biggest idiot, and I wanted to beg Michael to stay and referee.

Instead, I squeezed my husband and smiled. "I hope Doc Jones has someplace for me to elevate my feet."

Michael loaded the car while I looked around our bedroom one last time, tried to memorize being with him. For the next three weeks, he would work to pay for my crazy book-launch adventure. No more visits until the end of the Trace.

Twenty-one days. Two hundred and forty-eight miles.

Without my husband, it might as well have been infinity.

When I limped downstairs, I found Mom standing in the cabin's main room, her spring outfit accentuated with flawless hair and layers of matching jewelry. She strutted over and offered a bejeweled arm. "Do you need help getting to the car? I did extra workouts, you know. At the gym while Roy's been gone. I'm sure I can help you if you can't walk."

"Mom, I have to walk. I'm just stiff at the beginning." I ignored her outstretched arm and forced my legs to move. "I'll ride with Michael as far as Starkville."

"We got to get going! Doc Jones is—"

Michael helped me into his car and shut the door on Dad's rant. When he slipped next to me, he took my hand. "Whenever he gets like this, just remember what it feels like right now. Here. Holding my hand."

I didn't let go of Michael's hand until he left me. Red taillights swam like he receded underwater. I waved until I couldn't see him. Dad bumped my back and jolted me from my husband's side.

"Doc's a-waiting. We got to go."

As Mom drove through farmland south of Tupelo, I massaged my calves and longed for the Trace. Sunlight through leaves. The tangy scent of pine sap. Shadows on black water.

I listened to Dad delight Doc Jones with his own Trace stories, but I missed making my own. Five hours of walking was magical, if one saw enchantment in the ordinary. In spite of sore legs and frozen ankles, I was ready to spend five daily hours practicing the life I wanted to live.

In the meantime, Mom and I watched Dad laugh with his old friend, almost three hours without complaint. When I tottered to the car, Dad shook Doc's hand, and I wondered whether they would ever visit again.

I realized I gave Dad the gift of seeing people who mattered one more time.

We bumped toward Houston, Mississippi, Dad's voice interrupting my thoughts. "This next place. It have stairs?"

"Maybe Mom can carry you up the stairs, Dad. She offered to carry me to the car this morning."

Mom flicked her eyes in the rearview mirror. "Do you know that since I started going to the gym, I've lifted over a million pounds?"

"See, Dad? She can totally carry you upstairs."

When we pulled in front Bridges Hall Manor, we were laughing, familial music I never expected. Mom hauled things from the trunk while I circled the rambling Victorian and knocked on the front door. Before the echo died away, a woman who resembled Aunt Bee from the Andy Griffith Show greeted me. She took my hand, her sentences a whirlwind. "I'm Carol, and let me tell you, I've been waiting for you all day. I've got your room ready, because I know you're about to fall out, aren't you? And, oh! This must be your father. I've been reading all about you, Mr. Watkins, on Andra's website. I'm Carol Koutroulis."

Dad's chuckle shook his belly. "You been reading about me?"

"Yessir! I feel like I know you already." She waved Mom inside. "Mrs. Watkins, you just leave those things right there. I'll take care of unloading all that. Let's get this girl to bed."

I started to follow Carol up the carpeted stairway, but Dad's voice stopped us. "You got any rooms on the ground floor? I cain't do stairs."

"Dad—"

But Carol slipped past me and patted Dad's arm. "Oh, Mr. Watkins. I know better than that. Why, you've

single-handedly sold I-don't-know-how-many of Andra's books, haven't you? And you've driven all over half of Mississippi. And I saw where you took her to get that glorious fried chicken. You're one hearty fellow."

"You wouldn't believe I'm an eighty-year-old man, would you?"

Mom smiled behind her hand while Carol wove her spell. "Eighty? No. I'll never believe it."

When she tackled the stairs again, Dad was right behind her. "Yeah. I'm mighty spry for an old man, ain't I?"

Mom and I watched them ascend, their conversation drifting from the second floor. I leaned on the bannister and sighed. "I think we're in very good hands."

WALK LIKE AN EGYPTIAN
The Bangles

Mom couldn't sit still at the beginning of my third week. "I'm going to walk with you, Andra." She tied a green scarf under her chin and handed the car keys to Dad. He let them dangle from his fingers, like he was mystified by them.

I reached an arm around stooped shoulders and whispered, "Thanks for staying, Dad."

Seeing Mom and Dad together, I didn't know whether his decision to stay was sound. I was a shrieking shrew for suggesting the trip. My svelte, fit mother made Dad a wobbly old man. Substantial, but teetering. Almost ready to fall.

Mom watched him angle himself into the driver's seat. "I'm worried about your daddy, Andra."

Since I could remember, Mom started a third of her sentences with 'I'm worried about,' a habit I inherited and spent much of my adult life trying to break. Worry was a crutch for the mind, the worst outlet of the imagination. It was—

"Yeah. I am, too."

I couldn't hide what I felt on St. Patrick's Day. A week before my forty-fifth birthday. Dad shoulders drooped before my eyes. I worried he wouldn't make it to Nashville. Wondered whether he'd wake up the next morning

or stroke that afternoon. He gobbled sugary food and complained every time I made him move.

But I didn't have to tell Mom. She knew.

We were watching him die.

I stretched to banish worries, to combat Mom's harried thoughts. Even the happiest, healthiest people die a little every day.

Two hundred and ten miles of Mississippi behind me. Two hundred and thirty-four to go. I wondered why I hadn't met swamp creatures. Or been chased by Swamp Thing. For two weeks, my world was a Mississippi swamp.

Like my relationship with Mom. The surface read peaceful, but one never knew what lurked beneath the scrim of black water. What might fall fangs-first from twisted trees.

We fell apart over curtains, fabric that unraveled over a decade.

In 2001, Mom and Dad came for their inaugural visit to my new house, and they immediately took over.

"I thought I'd make you some curtains while I was here." Mom opened a bag and pulled out patterns and scraps of material. "I really like this dusty mauve color."

"Mom—"

She held it next to a window. "I've got a whole bolt in the car."

"Mom—"

"Let me get it, and we can see what it—"

"Mom, I don't want mauve curtains!"

She opened the garage door. "Oh, don't be silly, Andra. You'll love it."

I took the stairs two at a time. My bedroom. If I made it, I could figure out—

"What are you doing, Dad?" He was in my closet, fumbling through my color-coordinated skirt section. "None of that stuff fits you!"

He moved to my dresses. "I'm just making sure this wall is stable."

"You're looking for my files to find out what I paid

for this house! That's what you're doing!"

Dad's cackle of acknowledgement didn't stop his snoop session. He was my father; he thought he had a right to know everything.

Mom sauntered into the bedroom, trailing fabric. A bloody bridal train. "This will probably look better here, too. I don't really like those filmy curtains, and—"

"Get out! Getoutgetoutgetout!!!"

I pushed them onto the upstairs landing and banged the door closed. Mom's crime scene material seeped through the crack. I locked myself in the bathroom to avoid seeing the consequences of the thrust I made, the gash I inflicted.

It was my first attempt to be free.

I was thirty-two years old.

At the sink, I splashed cold water on my face. Water was water. Right?

When I went downstairs, Dad was gone, and Mom sat, straight-backed and wounded, in front of her sewing machine. She fingered a ragged corner of material and wouldn't look at me. "What's the matter with you, Andra? I thought we'd make curtains together, like we did—"

"That's the problem, Mom. You thought. You didn't ask me."

"But we had so much fun together at your other house all those years ago."

"Almost ten years ago, Mom. I was barely twenty-three then." I stalked around her, a wounded animal fighting for its turf.

"So? We're the same people. I still enjoy decorating with you."

My fist stung when I hit the table. "But you're not decorating with me. You're coming into my house—my house—and taking over."

Her cheeks glowed red. "But you've always liked me to take care of you, Andra. I thought—"

Thoughts. Her thoughts constricted my chest until I couldn't breathe.

I hated her.

The innocent way she always twisted circumstances

to fit her world view. Dogged conviction that her way was best. Her incessant need to define the woman I should be.

I couldn't exist that way anymore. Even if it meant destroying her.

"I don't need you to take care of me, Mother. I can take care of myself. Clearly. My house is even bigger than yours." She cowered in the chair, her fingers a blur of nervous energy, but I couldn't stop. "I don't want curtains. And if I ever decide I do, I'll pick them out myself. This is my house. My house! Do you hear me?"

More than a decade later, we stood together at milepost 210, in the heart of our own wasteland. Our Nowhere.

Mom buttoned her sequined sweater and adjusted her hat. "I've been going to the gym four hours every day for more than a year. I do seven miles on the treadmill. Surely, I can keep up with you."

"Okay, Mom. You win. You're in way better shape than me." I chewed my tongue and focused on stretching my calves. White flag flying, I surrendered to her will. "What's Dad gonna do while we walk?"

I stiff-walked his way, my feet and ankles refusing to loosen. "Dad! Mom's gonna walk with me. Just a few miles."

"Maybe all of it." She sidled up to me. Hand on hip. Face a made-up palette. She wore the look she employed when she required me to make my bed or eat some godawful thing.

"You can't walk fifteen miles, Linda."

I wanted to high-five Dad and shout, "Way to take one for the team! I'm so glad you said it." But I settled for a few moments of lightness to start my day.

"You're just jealous because you can't, Old Man." Mom didn't know much about baseball, but she was master of the verbal home run. She pranced up the road before he could argue. Cloudy eyes watched her.

"Well. I'll go on up to Line Creek and wait, I reckon."

"Just drive to milepost 212. See how Mom feels when she gets there."

Dad followed the rhythm of her retreating step. "But she's determined to walk with you the whole day."

"I know. But I have a feeling she might change her mind."

"I don't know. She's pretty stubborn, that woman. Kinda like you."

"See you, Dad."

I gimped away before Dad could remind me how much I was like my mother, because I didn't want to be like her. Impeccable coiffure in every situation. Always worried about appearances. Convinced she could exercise her way to immortality.

Behind her grace and flawless presentation, Mom was the most obstinate person I'd ever known.

My knee bones screeched together as I rattled up beside her. "I told Dad to go a couple of miles and wait."

"Why? I'm doing at least five miles today." She quickened her pace and kept a few steps ahead of me.

My ankles threatened to snap when I tried to match her, but Mom widened the gap. "If you can do fifteen, I can do at least half that."

I stopped next to an impressive ant hill. Tiny creatures zoomed along the ridge and penetrated multiple holes. Did they ever get tired of doing the same thing, day after day after day? Of having identical conversations?

Shaky breath rattled my rib cage. "I'm not going to—" But before I could finish, her hips shimmied ahead of me. I leaned over and put my hands on my knees. My feet already throbbed, and my hips wouldn't stop squeaking. "Mom, what I was trying to say is I'm not going to race you up the Trace. Nobody's timing this. We don't have to be anywhere."

"I'm not racing anybody." I could barely hear her, still pumping her legs at full speed.

Thirty minutes with my mother was an emotional slog through a week of fifteen mile days, but I redirected my thoughts to daffodils, daffodils, daffodils. I hobbled up beside her and put one hand on her arm. "I know you can do this faster than me, Mom. I concede defeat, because I'm really tired."

"Well, I can see how you would be. I just want to feel like I'm getting some exercise."

"I understand, but I decided last week that my walk

isn't a race. Hurrying to finish keeps me from experiencing the journey. I want to savor it, you know? See the colors change with the light and hear birds and animals and heed whispers in the breeze. Do you think we can do that? Just walk at a normal pace? And enjoy the quiet?"

Mom fixed the angle of her hat and retied the bow. "Of course. It'll give us a chance to talk."

"But I don't want to talk, Mom. I just want—"

"I heard what you said, Andra, but I don't see how you can stand all this quiet. It'd drive me crazy."

"It does. For a while. But a place can have a lot to say when we listen." I stepped into a reasonable pace, where I could breathe without panting, and Mom walked beside me. For blissful minutes, we were in sync. Sunlight streaked the road, and trees sprouted baby leaves. Hips and knees and ankles finally released. I relaxed, determined to begin my week with a positive outlook.

Until Mom sighed. One of her impatient I-can't-believe-I'm-being-asked-to-endure-this exhalations.

I gripped the edges of zen and turned to her. "All right, Mom. What do you want to talk about?"

Because Mom always had to talk. Until recent months, I avoided her phone calls, let them go to voicemail rather than listen to her yammering. When I told her I needed to go, she always responded with, "Okay. Did I tell you about….." Thirty minutes later, I shouted at her to hang up.

I couldn't stand the person I became during interminable conversations with my mother.

On the Trace, there was nowhere to go, no way to staunch the flow of words. No 'send to voicemail' button. I breathed into the Onslaught of Linda's Feelings.

"How's your daddy been?"

Well.

I didn't expect that.

"Why? Did you miss him? I thought you'd enjoy not having to listen to the blare of the television."

She twisted her rings. "I did enjoy it. For a few days. But one morning I got up, and I sat in the living room, and I said, 'It's too quiet'."

I laughed. "Yeah. Dad's world is pretty loud."

"That's because he can't hear a thing. But it was hard to be alone. I didn't realize how much I'd miss him. So, how's he been?"

"Oh, you know. An endless supply of strangers to talk to. Junk shops galore. Loves selling books. I think he got along okay with Alice." I stumbled over an ant hill and kicked the dirt. "It's just—"

"What?"

"Well, I never realized how weak he is, compared to a couple of years ago. I also didn't know about the, ah.........well, his toilet issues."

"He's gotten worse since his appendix ruptured. I worry so much, Andra. He's just like his sister was, right before she had her stroke."

My mind raced back to the worst night of the trip.

"Did I tell you about Dad's waking me up in the middle of the night?"

"He keeps me up every night, Andra. That sleep apnea machine......I hear it in my room. Well, your room. I sleep in your room now."

Does any child ever want to think about her parents sleeping together? Especially when that child knows what happens between her own sheets?

But my parents not sleeping together was another little death, an admission that a necessary part of their relationship was over. What was an adult child supposed to say to a parent who made that fragile concession?

I'm sorry?

You must be so relieved, because I don't know how you slept with all that noise for decades?

Do you miss sex?

Yuck.

I couldn't go there.

Cowardice found me instead. "There's Dad. Up ahead." The nose of the Mercury Grand Marquis jutted into the road adjacent to milepost 212.

"Oh, I've got at least two more miles in me. I'll tell Roy to go on."

I dug my heels into primordial dirt. "Wait. Before we get to Dad, I need to tell you something."

Mom walked a few steps and stopped. Dad doddered from trees, several rolls of toilet paper stuffed under one arm. Even from a distance, I saw the stain along the butt crease of his khaki pants. "Oh, Roy......." Mom whispered.

"Dad's not doing well, is he?"

"Well, he is eighty. And overweight. His nutritionist told him the other day, 'If it tastes good, Roy, don't eat it.' Which just makes him more determined to make bad choices, as I'm sure you've seen."

I stared at my father, the person who was larger than weakness, bigger than pain. Before he got into the car, he wheeled toward the woods, tearing another roll of toilet paper from the dwindling pack.

"I had to help him off the sofa the other night. He couldn't even get up to go to the bathroom."

"I told him he needs to do more to strengthen his legs, but I don't know, Andra. He's a Watkins."

"What does that mean?"

"Those Watkinses, they don't like to push themselves."

I was a Watkins, and I pushed myself. Every damn day. Just like Meriwether Lewis. I showed up every day. On schedule. And I forced pulpy feet another fifteen miles. And another. And another.

I loosened my sandals to let my toes breathe. "I guess I'm not a Watkins, then."

Mom took in my distended, bandage-swaddled toes. "No, you're not. You get this crazy determination from me."

I ground my teeth through the torture of standing, and envisioned what it must be like for Dad. Every day. All the time. "But what happens when he really can't get up, Mom? What do we do then?"

I touched her shoulder, but she shrugged beyond the weight. Like she could sidestep the looming situation with Dad. She crossed the highway and waved. "Roy! I'm going to do a couple more miles with Andra! Is that all right?"

Dad shambled through trees, two rolls of toilet paper lighter. "Okay. I'll just drive on up the road, to......what? There a parking lot up that way, Andra?"

"I don't know, Dad. You've got the map."

"Huh?"

"The map! Look at the map."

"Oh. Right." He opened the back door. Toilet rolls unspooled like party streamers. He emerged with his full map of the Natchez Trace Parkway. It cascaded open, a waterfall of paper. I tried not to notice his pant stains or the stink.

"Ain't no restrooms in this whole stretch today."

"Well, that isn't stopping you from turning the Trace into an outdoor potty party, is it?"

My joke was a stinker. Nobody laughed.

Dad crumpled the map. "I'll just drive on up the road, Linda. When I see a place to pull off, I will. And you can decide what you want to do when you get there."

"Don't go too far, Roy. I mean, I'm fine, but, well...........you might need me before I'm ready to quit for the day."

He tugged the seat of his pants and studied his feet. "That's right. I might." After he winched his way into the driver's seat, he started the car and pulled onto pavement.

When I was sure he couldn't see us in the rearview mirror, I whirled on Mom. "Just what are you two not telling me?"

"We tell you everything, Andra." She toggled her hat and turned her back on me.

GREEN ONIONS

Booker T & the MGs

I remember the first time I messed my pants. I mean, not the very first time, you understand. But the first time I did it in front of other people.

I was a six-year-old boy, riding the bus home from school, and I got this powerful gas. Musta been something my mother put in my lunch, or the consequences of dipping into her snuff. Whatever it was, it needed to get out.

I looked around that bus and figured we was a bunch of kids. All kids stink. I never climbed on that bus without getting my nostrils full of smells. All stale sweat and dirty bodies and rotten food.

So I thought I could pass a little wind, and nobody'd know the difference. It'd just blend with the other stuff.

Only it wasn't just air that came out.

Well, I didn't know what to do.

Them kids started pinching their noses together, and looking around, and climbing all over the seats, "Who tooted? Where's the baby who messed their pants? We don't got no diapers in elementary school, baby. Here, tootie-tootie-tootie."

And I was right there with 'em. It was only a little bit. I couldn't see no stain. I figured it'd be all right to pretend, 'til I could get off that bus and run home to my momma.

Everything changed at the end of our dirt road. I stepped into sunshine, and them kids all figured out it was me. I

run off, with them screaming, "Hey, Tootie! Better bring your diapers to school tomorrow! You sure do stink!"

Andra had the same problem, all through elementary school, especially around the time she started that womanly business. I sat in the den and listened to Linda in the bathroom, telling Andra how to wash right, to make sure she used soap. I wanted to go in there and tell 'em both, "She gets this from me. She'll figure it out eventually."

Because I did. Until my old body gave out. On that bus, I never thought I'd have the same problem seventy-some years later. When we're young, we can't imagine being old. But then, sometime in our forties or fifties, when our bodies break down, we get scared. When am I gonna keel over from a heart attack? Golly molly, if I have a stroke, I hope it's massive enough to kill me. Is this bump cancer?

It's only when we start to fag out that we realize the things we took for granted are the ones we don't want to live without. A full set of teeth. Hair that grows where it's supposed to. The bulge that wakes a fella up in the middle of the night. A body that can make it to a toilet before the crap starts coming.

Guess folks can start calling me Tootie again.

WALKIN' AFTER MIDNIGHT
Patsy Cline

"I don't understand why my ankle hurts." Mom dragged her leg like a wounded animal. At milepost 257, the Trace transformed into a commuter highway. We dodged morning traffic and illegal eighteen wheelers on the outskirts of Tupelo, birthplace of Elvis Presley.

For three days, Mom started and ended my walks with me. Four or five miles at the beginning. Two or three at the end. We eased into conversations, two grown-ups building a symphony. When notes clashed, we erased them and tried again. And again. With miles of nowhere to go, we uncovered lifetimes to discuss.

I was surprised when I found myself relishing hours one-on-one with my mother. After a decade of shouted battles and seething skirmishes, I embraced the possibility of peace.

Another eighteen wheeler cut short our conversation. The sky whirled as we tumbled down an embankment. I popped to my feet and scrabbled up the hill. "You're not supposed to be on the Trace!" I shouted and waved my fists. Backdraft flattened us. *No Commercial Vehicles.* I pointed to a sign and helped Mom stand. "Are you all right?"

She finger-combed brown hair and repositioned her hat. "If you are, I am, too." But her pinched face wove another story. She favored one leg and winced whenever she put weight on the other.

Hands on hips, I blocked her progress. "Okay, Mom. Describe the pain in your ankle."

She stood on one leg and wiggled her foot. Back and forth. Side to side. Whenever her Achilles tendon stretched along the back of her leg, she grimaced but turned it into a smile. "It sort of burns in my heel. I thought it was fine this morning, but it started again after I took a few steps."

First, Dad needed diapers. Then, Mom couldn't walk. I was the worst person ever for guilting them into an adventure with me.

Like Meriwether Lewis preparing for his Western expedition, I studied possible ailments I was likely to encounter during my thirty-four day slog. I googled repetitive motion injuries. What caused them. Who was most at risk.

Continuous movement. Unforgiving surfaces. Age. Mom was a repetitive motion trifecta.

"Tendonitis. That's what you have, Mom."

"What's that?" She lunged forward, her injured heel stretched flat behind her.

"Don't do that! Stretching those tendons will only inflame them more."

"But I thought I was supposed to stretch a sore muscle."

"Tendonitis isn't a sore muscle, Mom. All this walking has put too much stress on your tendons, and—"

"But I walk seven miles a day at the gym!"

I scrubbed my hands over my sweaty face. Why did my mother always have to be obstinate to the point of madness? I prepared to unsheathe my response. Stubbornness was the very quality that had me standing next to a traffic-clogged highway in northern Mississippi. Why I couldn't discard my dream of living from the written word. Orneriness was the signature of my DNA.

I couldn't point fingers at her.

I breathed in alluvial dust and asked millions of Trace spirits for patience.

"Mom." My even voice startled me, but I pressed on. "The motion of a treadmill isn't like walking on a paved road. The machine distributes the stress on your joints and makes the workout less taxing. Not less effective. Just easier on your body. Does that make sense?"

She gimped along the grass, her back to me. "Oh, I'm sure I can just walk this off. Let's keep going."

I bit my lip and counted to ten. On nine, I saw the nose of the Mercury. It jutted into the road five hundred yards ahead. "There's Dad. I think you should stop when we get to the car."

"But—"

"No buts. If it's tendonitis, walking will only make it worse. You need elevation, ice and rest."

"There's no time for all that. I've got to get your supper. And take care of Roy. And—"

My mother. When I was growing up, I basked in Mom's waiting on me. Of her buying me something new, never realizing she went without. Of her arranging her existence around taking me where I wanted. I thought she did those things because she loved me.

In part, I was wrong.

Mom needed to be needed.

For much of my adult life, she was happiest when I wasn't happy, but she wasn't a sadist who liked to watch me suffer. My agonies gave her something to do. A place to be. A role to play.

I needed her when I struggled.

Until I didn't. My not-needing her was the fuse that detonated our relationship. We spent a decade piling shards of hurt into fortresses, and we camped behind walls, hurling nuclear invective. I didn't understand Mom's need to be needed.

Neither did she. For years, she swore she wasn't needy and hung up when I insisted she was.

But, a few months before my walk, something shifted. I called her one day and caught her reading my novel. When she finished, she told me it was good. Really good.

I couldn't remember the last time Mom offered me

unsolicited praise.

When I asked Mom to join us for three weeks on the Trace, she resisted. How could she go to the gym? Who would pay the bills? Would their empty house be a target for thieves?

As Dad and I planned, Mom worried. The more she heard about my walk, the more convinced she was that Dad and I would kill each other. When she decided to come, I uncovered my hope candle and let it shine. She knew exactly what I needed.

And I understood her. I put my arm around her thin shoulders. "Mom, you can still take care of me. You know what would really make me happy right now?"

"What?" Firelight flared behind her eyes.

"A real latte. I haven't had one in almost two weeks. Will you go into Tupelo? See if they have a Starbucks?"

She staggered to the car at milepost 259. "All right. If you're sure you'll be okay alone."

"Mom, I've done most of this alone." I stuck my head through an open window. "Dad! Make sure Mom gets some ice for her ankle, okay?"

"Huh? What for?"

"Just make sure."

"Why you quitting so soon, Linda?" Mom opened the driver's door and shooed Dad from her seat, the wheelhouse of control.

They motored toward Tupelo and left me beside a pasture dotted with cows. Ragged edges of barbed wire ringed the perimeter, next to a brown sign. *Chickasaw Village Site. 1 mile.* "People wandered in and out of that place for decades. For centuries. Maybe even for millennia." In forgotten times, did children struggle against parents for control of their lives? Did they live long enough to witness the body's sickening decline?

Thirty minutes later, I sat on a fence and sipped my latte. Long-dead ghosts hovered in an expanse of field, a vacant reminder of the town that once thrived there. I listened for stories embedded in the breeze. In my whispered thoughts, I asked them one question.

Were any of them like my parents and me?

A MILLION MILES AWAY
David Byrne

Less than a mile into a new day, a guy waved me to his white truck. Surveyors sprayed the road with orange hieroglyphics. Dots and circles. Dashes and arrows. The bearded man made a note on a clipboard. "I'm the federal inspector on this job. Road's closed up ahead. These boys here tell me you're walking the Trace."

"Yep."

"How far you come?"

"All the way from Natchez."

He clocked the milepost across the highway. "Two-seventy. Damn. You've walked all that way?"

"Yes."

"By yourself?"

"Pretty much."

"On the parkway?"

I pushed red hair under my hat and nodded. "There's nowhere else to walk."

He scratched his salt-and-pepper beard and whistled. "Nobody does that." Avoiding my eyes, he concentrated on his paperwork. I could almost hear cogs turning in his brain. Let me go ahead? Or tell me I couldn't?

After a few beats, he turned to me. "Technically, the

road's closed. I should make you get off the highway. You know, follow the official detour." He pounded the steering wheel a final time. "But I get what you're doing. I mean, I don't really, but I do, if that makes sense?"

"It doesn't make much sense to me, either." Relief whooshed through my lips. I'd been holding my breath.

His eyes crinkled at the corners when he laughed. "All right. They're resurfacing a bridge. Should be almost done. I'll radio up ahead and tell them to let you through. Only got one side blocked, so they can hold traffic, and you can walk across. Okay?"

"Thank you!" I shouted as he drove away. How many bureaucratic rules and regulations had he broken to keep my walk intact?

I hiked next to black Mississippi earth, wet and aching to be plowed. The ground vibrated with the thrum of unseen machinery. I wished Mom was with me, but I ordered her to stay at Bridges Hall and ice her ankle. When men needed to be charmed, she could always out-flirt me.

Dad materialized and steered the Mercury half on tarmac and half off. "You can't go that way, Andra. They done said."

"You pull into the road up there and watch me."

"I already been up there, and they told me you can't walk it."

I hooked my fingers into my backpack straps and stood taller. "Well, maybe I'm more convincing than you, Old Man."

Challenge combusted behind his eyes. He revved the engine, and his hands vibrated on the wheel, like he could absorb mechanical power. "I bet you I'll sell 'em all books before you get there, and I'll be waiting to drive you around. They done told me where to go." He peeled away and blew the horn before I raised his bet.

Some relationships worked best with good-natured sparring. Even as a child, I questioned my father. Demanded to know why he was right and

 I was wrong. Dad's brown eyes sparkled to life when I argued with him, and his deep-throated chuckle always ended our rows.

I didn't understand the flaw in Dad's lessons on interacting with men until I was in my thirties. While Dad

taught me to push boundaries, to express my opinions, to stand up for myself, he never explained the male ego. Nothing I said to Dad was below the belt. It took almost two decades of adult mistakes to learn some men didn't respect strong women.

In fact, a few men feared them.

At milepost 271, Dad pulled into the side road and winched himself from the car, my green-swaddled novel in each hand. Before I took a step, he flagged down a car as it slowed to a stop sign and launched into his sales pitch.

I wished I could be that confident. Dad knew my book was good, and he hadn't even read it. Why couldn't I believe in myself the way he believed in me?

By the time I reached the intersection, Dad sold books to two customers, stalled in their effort to turn north and follow the Trace. He beckoned me to the eastern side of the highway and dragged me to their window. "These people here's from Louisiana, but they got a house up this way. I sold them some books, and you need to sign 'em."

Road dust was sandpaper on swollen fingers when I held a pen, but I smiled and made small talk. Where they were from. How often they drove a highway older than Time. What they thought of Meriwether Lewis.

When they left, Dad grabbed my shoulders and maneuvered me toward the car. "You got to sign more of these books, Andra. I can't sell 'em without them being signed."

My fingers throbbed from one bout with a pen. No matter how much I trained, I was never prepared for the toll of gravity. Five hours of swinging my arms caused blood to pool in my fingers. By the end of a fifteen mile day, they wouldn't bend. Clumsy numbness invaded my hands for hours after I finished, making the simplest tasks a challenge. I blotted my face with my sleeve and sighed. "I'll sign a few more tonight, Dad."

He flung the back door open. "No. Now. While I drive you around this construction."

"But I don't have to drive around the construction.

They already told me I could walk through it."

He studied the cloud of tar dust, the choreography of equipment. "You ain't walking through that. I won't let you. One of them things could run over you."

I picked up a pen and scribbled my name. "I am walking through that, and I won't get hurt." I handed him a stack of signed books. But as I prepared my diatribe about how many years I'd taken care of myself, I chomped my lips. Dad would worry about me for as long as he breathed. Probably after he was dead. Worry was the essence of loving something he had a hand in creating.

And, if Life taught me anything about worry, the best antidote was diversion. Distraction. Dragging the mind to another place.

I squeezed his arm. "You've got enough signed books to get you through today. Since you're not selling too many."

"What? I'll show you not selling too many!" He was behind the wheel and gone before I took a step toward the construction zone, danger from heavy equipment forgotten.

Younger than he'd been in days.

I scrubbed grime off my face and hoped my eyes weren't too swollen. Men in neon vests buzzed next to machines, a lone flagger at their front. I sized him up like a sniper plotting the destruction of a target.

"Hi." I fluttered lashes caked with road grease and hoped it resembled mascara. Maybe the red blotches on my fair cheeks mimicked blush.

Who was I kidding?

I shoved my self-doubt aside and smiled. "The inspector said you'd let me walk through."

The man took in my dirty green jacket. My sandals swaddled with duct tape. Streaks of dingy hair glued to facial filth. He leaned on his Slow sign.

 "You the girl who's walking the Trace?"

"That's me."

"I been hearing about you, but damn. I thought you'd be some butch she-man."

What did that mean? Feminine women couldn't accomplish feats of endurance?

I stood straighter. "I really appreciate your letting me walk through the construction site."

"Oh. Yeah." He grabbed his walkie-talkie. "I got a lady here. She's gonna walk your way."

"A what?"

"A lady. In a green jacket. I need you to hold traffic and let her walk through."

Radio silence ticked through seconds. "She hot? This lady?"

"Come on, man." He cut his eyes sideways.

"Well? Am I?"

If laughter is the great uniter, we bonded. We were still laughing when he clicked his radio and said, "Just hold traffic, okay? And let her walk through."

He waved me into a sulfur cloud, and I plunged in before he could change his mind. My teeth knocked together when my foot hit the overpass. As I hurried along the empty lane, every worker tipped a hard hat. The other flagger awaited me at the end, a line of cars and campers snaking behind him. He waved me over. "You got another bridge like this one. 'Bout a half mile ahead. I tole 'em you was coming."

"Thank you!" I took a few steps and snapped a picture of Trace improvements.

It took almost three hundred miles to encounter an improvement project. The federal government diverted funds from its eighth-most-visited National Park, because few people would protest. Bigger populations lobbied for restricted funds, while I walked over swaths of pavement missing white-and-yellow lines, stepped around open potholes and photographed acres of discarded trash. The Natchez Trace remained a version of Nowhere, forgotten by those who were supposed to preserve it.

But as I inched my way closer to the Meriwether Lewis site in Tennessee, I only cared about one thing. Congress cut ranger patrols, closed restrooms and left many Trace stops forlorn, but I started my walk knowing

Meriwether Lewis's grave might be closed.

Would it be open the day I got there?

At the end of almost two miles of construction, I expected to find Dad gloating, "I sold all them books! Who's the best salesman, huh?"

The Trace stretched northward, barren. A world emptied of my father. How I would miss him when he was gone. Emptiness tripped me, sent me reeling. On my knees, I scrolled through my Trace time with Dad. I tried to record snatches of conversation for play back when I ached for our banter, but he always froze. He would force me to remember.

But Memory wouldn't be enough to capture him.

People forget the nuances of a voice. Photographs smear lines. I practiced Dad's speech patterns by writing them, and I mocked his voice and mannerisms. But I'd never be able to conjure him. The well of memory wasn't deep enough to remake a person.

I brushed grass from my pants and stumbled into another sign.

Old Trace. 1/2 mile.

The Old Trace was an earthy gash, eroded remnants of the original trail. I sought out those strips of sunken dirt. Hollows amplified the echo of Time. A stampeding herd of buffalo. The thwack of arrow against bow. A lone boatman, surprised by a thief, pounded to death for his treasure.

I never wanted to hear him scream.

But I rocked back and forth, stomach and bladder insisting upon my full attention. "I'm sure a bathroom is too much to hope for," I mumbled and tramped into the empty parking lot. Splinters pricked my fingers at the faded brown-and-gold information sign. A bannister drew me to uneven stairs. I readied my lunch on a picnic table tattooed with graffiti.

My bladder twinged again. I hopped down stairs and sprawled on the leaf-strewn Old Trace. Branches blocked clouds and sky. I wondered

whether Meriwether Lewis rode that far south. If he ever walked where I stood.

My phone jangled. Ghosts whirlpooled through dead leaves in retreat.

"Hello?"

"Andra?" Dad's voice boomed over the speaker. "Where are you?"

"I'm at Old Trace. Old Trace!"

"We just drove by there. Didn't see nobody."

"I was...........um............" How did I tell my father I was communing with the past? With the whispers I heard? Walking fifteen miles alone made me sensitive to spirits swirling in layers. After almost three weeks, their voices wafted along zephyrs blown from the beginning of Time. The Natchez Trace kept me company, and its haunting brought lonesome joy.

Even though my experience was true, it sounded crazy. I stumbled over words. "I............."

"Well, I just sold another book. That makes twelve today."

"That's great, Dad."

"Yeah. So, me and your mother'll turn around and come back. Didn't see you when we rode by. Can't figure out why."

I hauled myself from the Old Trace. From where I stood, my view of the highway was blocked by trees. I dropped my pants and squatted. Just adding my essence to history.

Another way wandering souls marked their territory.

Mom and Dad squealed into the parking lot. Before the car stopped, Mom fled the driver's seat. "I think I'll walk with you for a while today, Andra. I called Roy to come and get me, because I'm all better. Sitting around that B and B with ice on my foot was making me stir crazy."

"Mom, you haven't rested your ankle enough." Banana squished between my cheeks.

"I iced it! All morning!"

"Dad!" I joined him at the information sign. "Tell Mom she can't walk with me."

Rather than answer, Dad whipped out his manhood and sprayed the ground around my feet.

I jumped from the path of the yellow stream and almost dropped my banana. "Eewww! Dad!"

Mom snickered. "Well, he obviously can't judge whether I'm fit to walk. He's got so much gas today,

and—"

"Please, Mom. I'm eating." I stalked back to what remained of my lunch. Peanut butter became sawdust in my mouth. "I don't think you should—"

Mom assumed a stance I recognized as part of my genetic code. Hands on hips. Weight on one leg. A tone that brokered no debate. "I'm going, Andra. I can't stand to be cooped up anymore. With him."

A final yellow rivulet ran to the sign's base. Dad shook himself dry and zipped up. He reached into a pocket and found a sleeve of peanuts. After he dumped a salty pile into his palm, he offered it to me. "Want some?"

I took a few steps backward and almost fell over the picnic table. "Pee-seasoned nuts? No thanks, Dad. You enjoy that."

He was already popping peanuts into his mouth. "You see this tree?" He pointed to a moss-covered pine. "It's probably a few hundred years old."

"That's great, Dad."

"Some amazing wood along this place. Make some mighty fine tables."

"You already bought a table, Dad." I gestured to the Mercury's trunk, where his prize took up precious real estate amid flats of water, hiking gear and protein snacks. Nobody could convince him we didn't have room for an antique table. If Dad took a shine to a piece of junk, he always found a way to bring it home.

"I can sell it." He sauntered over to Mom and me. "It's the mark you leave on stuff. You know, refinishing it and whatnot. Lets people know you been here."

I excavated memory. I found my first antique in a barn, along the banks of a muddy river. A dresser of light oak, stained brass highlighting its three drawers. When I put my ear along its pockmarked top, I heard music. The clash of an iron skillet and crackling fire.

Maybe everything held the record of what came before it.

EVERY DAY IS A WINDING ROAD
Sheryl Crow

I remember the first time I bought an old piece of furniture. Linda and me was just married, and we didn't have much money. But I knew she liked finery even then, so I took her up to the furniture store and told her to pick out some things. I gave her a budget and all that, but of course she went over. Picked out a house full of too-much-what-all.

When the delivery truck groaned into our driveway, I watched 'em unload. Chairs and tables and a green-and-cream sofa that'd seat five. White lamps that was shaped like the bulb of an onion.

I waited and waited.

For a mattress.

And maybe a bed.

At the end of the whole shiny parade, I turned to Linda. "Well, you got all this dining room stuff, and the living room's packed to the gills, and I appreciate you getting me that tan chair, but where's the bed?"

She ran delicate fingers along one of them lamps. "Bed? Oh, Roy. I guess I saw these lamps, and I forgot all about the bedroom. I love these so much. Don't you?"

"How much was they?"

Well, when she told me, I knew we wouldn't be going back to the furniture store anytime soon. Linda'd done gone and blew our furniture budget for the entire year.

I started poking around junk places and talking to folks. Before long, I found a Jenny Lind bed, one of them wood head-and-foot boards with the knotty spindles. It was caked with white paint, but underneath was solid walnut. Being a wood man, I could tell when I scratched it a little. I bought it for five dollars and took it home to refinish myself.

Linda hated it on sight. "Roy Watkins, I am not sleeping on that piece of trash."

"Just you wait, Linda. I'll make this thing the best bed you ever seen."

I bought a bunch of refinishing supplies and got to it. Took me almost a week working nights to strip all that white paint off. I repaired a couple of them broke spindles and varnished it. When I was done, I set it up in our bedroom.

It was the prettiest thing in our house. Even Linda had to agree. When Andra came along, we gave that bed to her. She's still got it, set up in her and Michael's place. Sleeps better than any bed I ever had.

Every piece of junk's got a beautiful soul. It just takes the right person to coax it out.

WALKING ON SUNSHINE
Katrina and the Waves

Morning sun streaked the pavement as Michael and I ambled along the north-to-south side of the Natchez Trace Parkway. Milepost 301. The start of my forty-fifth birthday. Mississippi Hill Country gave way to pre-Alabama waterways and plains. Michael's visit was a birthday surprise he planned before I started walking.

He always believed I would finish, though I still wavered. Wherever he caught me with a cell signal, Michael used FaceTime to encourage, to console, and to tell me how much he loved me. He never questioned my choice to walk 444 miles alone. Never voiced his fears. Never complained about five weeks apart. I gripped his palm and willed myself to be the strength he saw in me.

To mirror his strength.

I pulled Michael to a stop and snapped a picture of a discarded toothbrush. People doing seventy in cars didn't notice trash. It couldn't compete with the storied scenery. But on foot, I saw it everywhere, neglected bits of humanity tossed along a forgotten roadway.

Much like Meriwether Lewis. He returned from his conquest of the West, more famous than Katy Perry or Lady Gaga. Desired for his company. Celebrated.

Until he died of two gunshot wounds on Tennessee's Natchez Trace.

On the eve of his thirty-second birthday, he penned an expedition journal entry:

> This day I completed my thirty-first year, and conceived that I had in all human probability now existed about half the period which I am to remain in this Sublunary world. I reflected that I had as yet done but little, very little indeed, to further the hapiness of the human race, or to advance the information of the succeeding generation. I viewed with regret the many hours I have spent in indolence, and now soarly feel the want of that information which those hours would have given me had they been judiciously expended. But since they are past and cannot be recalled, I dash from me the gloomy thought and resolved in future, to redouble my exertions and at least indeavour to promote those two primary objects of human existance, by giving them the aid of that portion of talents which nature and fortune have bestoed on me; or in future, to live for mankind, as I have heretofore lived for myself.

While some historians called the paragraph a foreshadowing of his supposed suicide, I interpreted it as the personal challenge of an ambitious man who wanted to be remembered for his contributions to mankind. How many times had I admonished myself to try harder, to give more, to do better? Did wanting to grow as a human being and chiding myself when I didn't make me suicidal?

As much as he hoped to be remembered, his reticence for self-exposure and his murky death make him hard to know. And I always went for men who were hard to know, though I never understood why.

On my birthday, I wasn't thinking about the famous explorer. Meri-wether Lewis was days ahead of me, buried under a broken shaft of granite near Hohenwald, Tennessee. I only considered the next fifteen miles. It was easier to skip along behind my husband and admire his butt in hiking pants.

"Do you know how good you look in those—" I froze near milepost 309.

Michael whirled on me. "What is it?"

Silver glittered at my feet. I stooped to retrieve a thin disc, lodged between white line and grass.

William Clark's immortal words shouted through Time.

Ocean in view! O! The Joy!

"A Lewis and Clark nickel. It was tails up. Right here." I pointed to the inch of pavement. Clark's joy flooded my heart as I held it aloft and squealed, "It's a birthday present. From Meriwether Lewis to me."

"No way." Michael took the chewed-up nickel and inspected its rough edges, its tire-worn surfaces.

I flipped the coin to block fantastical explanations.

Because it would just be crazy.

Meriwether Lewis's haunting of my life was mythic in our household. When I woke my husband one night, claiming to have heard a man in our bedroom chanting, "You have the complete story," Michael didn't question my sanity. He tolerated my tears for a man long dead, my talks with a ghost I couldn't love, my stalking of a spirit I'd never contain.

My husband understood me. He knew my soul.

The nickel reinforced my clarity. It was a sign of my mind's power to shape Life.

Before I started my trek, I packed a zip-lock bag of good luck charms. I sat across from Michael at our shared desk, and I scrutinized each item. Cards from readers. A two-dollar bill. A buckeye foraged from a riverbank.

And a pristine Lewis and Clark nickel.

"What are you going to do with that?" Michael asked as I crammed everything into a plastic shroud.

"This nickel?" Sunlight sparkled on its surface. "I'm going to leave it on Lewis's grave. You know, as a thank you. Or something. I don't know. I'll figure it out when I get there."

Michael flashed a lopsided smile. "Or he will."

"What?"

"Nothing." He resumed whatever he was doing. I couldn't coax him to talk about my nickel again.

Until my birthday.

He cupped the roadside talisman in his palm. "Do you think he knew?"

"Knew what?" My fingers shook as I took it. On the Parkway map, we were a day's walk from Colbert Ferry, a stand on the Tennessee River just south of the Alabama/Tennessee state line. Many historians believed Lewis first stepped on the Natchez Trace in northern Mississippi. I looked at Michael, my skeptic husband, whose only faith rested in me. "Do you think this means Lewis was here?"

Michael closed his hands around mine, enveloping the nickel between us. "He must have, Andra. After all we've been through with his story, I don't doubt this is some sort of message from him."

"But—"

"What?"

Possibilities swirled through my mind. Was the nickel his blessing of the new ending I made for him?

I unzipped a pocket and slipped the nickel inside. "This has to be a birthday present from Lewis." I twirled metal between my fingers. "Why else would it be right here? On this day? With you to witness it?"

I studied how the earth sloped upward to trees. When I closed my eyes, I listened. For hoofbeats on root-bound dirt. For shouts of men who'd lost a horse. For the deal that sent Lewis ahead while James Neely, a Chickasaw Indian agent, stayed behind. I sniffed the air for moonshine. For evidence of the insanity so many historians claimed Lewis carried with him to Grinder's Stand.

But all I had was a nickel.

 I clutched it, and I sighed. When I started out to weave a final story of Meriwether Lewis, I never expected him to participate.

Yet, he did.

Another sign magnified my bliss.

State Line. 1/2 Mile.

A brown sign with gold lettering, shaped like a shield. For almost four weeks, signs marked the progress of my life. I trekked through swamps, across forests, along the hills of Mississippi. More than three hundred miles of capricious weather. Sleet. Wind. Tornado scares. Pelting rain and blistering sunshine.

Michael squeezed my hand. When I looked at him, my heart swam in his blue eyes. He touched my cheek. "How do you feel?"

Emotions rendered me mute. How did I think I'd feel when I walked the length of a state? Elated? Confused? Exhausted? It all frothed inside me, competing for prominence, but elation burbled to the top. If I could walk across the length of a whole state, I knew I could do anything.

I hurried along the road, toward another sign.

Bear Creek Mound.

A remnant of a forgotten civilization, one of many along the Trace. Almost a thousand years old.

I visited it the year before. Michael and I approached Bear Creek Mound from the other direction, a scouting trip for my novel. We drove into the empty parking lot and ambled through the field. When I wandered beside the mound, I heard a scream buried in the wind.

Another character bursting through history to claim her place in my story.

When I stared southward that day, I wondered what was there but never thought I would walk the length of that mystery. The Natchez Trace was a portal to the past. It didn't reveal the future.

I turned to Bear Creek Mound. A little boy shrieked across the field. When he reached the grassy hill, he climbed the dirt and jumped along the sunken top. I snapped picture after picture. I didn't hear his parents when they called him, wasn't conscious of their departure.

I was lost in the story of a different child.

Me.

Wondering whether my father would've stopped to let me run free.

My life mirrored Dad's journeys in the car. His obsession with Time. "We made good time." Or, "We could've made better time." The measure of Time was always Dad's first announcement once we arrived at our destination. Like the journey was a NASCAR race against numbers on a clock.

Was that why I always blasted through everything? I never took time to stop, to look, to savor.

Maybe my Trace adventure altered that dynamic for Dad and me, fifteen mile increments at a time. While Dad inspected every small-town junk shop and lingered with strangers, I memorized crimps in pavement, explored geographic layers and met hundreds of birds. I looked forward to Dad's stories about his days. Who he met. How he sold books. Even what he ate.

Schedules were irrelevant in the face of waning Time.

"Are you ready?" Michael walked a few steps ahead of me. Toward another sign. I couldn't see its face, but I knew what it proclaimed.

I dragged my feet through Mississippi grass, a state that fed me, housed me and embraced me for twenty-four days. Its people exuded hospitality, charm and backbones of steel. Innkeepers flamed with passion for the Natchez Trace, and they were untiring in their efforts to showcase it, even if it meant struggling in places few people stopped. I dreaded every goodbye.

"Let me take a couple more pictures." I listened to the burble of Bear Creek. A few steps, and Mississippi would be a memory. Relationships and nuances I wanted to recall but would never remember in Life's compression of details to highlights.

I handed my phone to Michael and surveyed the rusted stays of the brown road sign, tall enough to stand underneath. *Entering Alabama.* I hung onto metal posts and straddled two states.

And I smiled. Open-mouthed wonder at my accomplishment.

"I did it. I walked across an entire state. Me. By myself."

Voices fanned the flames of rapture. "We always knew you could. Because we did."

I breathed them in. To carry them through northwestern Alabama. Across the heart of Tennessee. All the way to my Nashville finish line.

When I took Michael's hand, I didn't look back. Finished wasn't done. To be finished was bittersweet, like I didn't want it to end, but it had to. To be done meant I was through with Mississippi, but that could never be. It seeped into my heart, its landscape spangled with images of my father. Laughing with strangers in roadside restaurants. Buying furniture he didn't need. Selling books to folks who never intended to buy. My walk became an endless parade of gifts.

I found joy in claiming them.

I'M WALKIN'

Fats Domino

Alabama started its only full day with a raindrop. It splashed my eye and jarred my contact. While I worked my eyelid to push it into place, Mom cranked the Mercury Grand Marquis. "I wish I felt like walking with you today, Andra, but my ankle still hurts. I guess I'm stuck with your daddy."

Dad poked his head through the open car window. "We'll go find you a snack and check out that Iuka place. What kinda name for a town is that? Iuka, Mississippi?" His laughter reverberated through silence when they left me. I pondered a soaked stretch of roadway near milepost 315.

Skeletal pain sizzled through my legs and feet. My muscles were frayed rubber bands before the weak bits snapped. Determined to find the day's gift, I turned my ravaged body northward. "Alabama, be kind to me."

Less than forty miles of the Natchez Trace cut through the northwestern corner of Alabama, riddled with watersheds that dumped into the Tennessee River and crisscrossed rich farmland. I wiped more rain from my eyes and left the first milepost. "It's just rain. Only my face will suffer."

Along the ridge line, wet seeped into my waterproof jacket and pants. It cascaded down my legs and into my shoes. Sleety rain beat a steady rhythm on the road, and it carried voices in every plop and smack.

"My leather shoes fell apart by the time I walked this

far, and I had to make it to Tennessee on bare feet."

"I'd give anything for that fancy stuff you're wearing. Skins leak, you know."

"Do you people ever think about how good you have it? All your complaining about the state of your feet. You don't know pain, girlie."

Boatmen. Delirious and showy. Broken and extreme. I turned my face downwind and shouted, "I'm still here. Doing what you did. I'm a girl, and I'm proud! Walking by myself, which beats your packs of skittish men. Leave me the hell alone! You hear me?"

Clouds parted, and the wintry mix fled. My knees groaned into a valley, but I stepped lighter, convinced my will could change the weather.

In a treeless expanse of fields, a horn broke my reverie.

"Andra!" Dad waved me to his window. "Got you a snack."

I rolled my eyes at salted peanuts. "I've got nuts in my backpack, Dad. More nuts in my protein bars. You just got these because you wanted them."

"You know your daddy." Mom talked over Dad's protests.

"I got 'em for you."

"You did not, Dad."

"I did! But if you really don't want 'em............" He tore into the bag and dumped them into his mouth.

I pulled windblown hair from mine. "Wind's picking up. But looks like it's done raining. I hope that means I've made it through the worst of it."

"Iuka. That was the worst of it." Mom fiddled with her rings and scowled. "I can't wait to go home."

"Really, Mom? You're not enjoying this together time?"

She diverted her attention beyond her window, while Dad exclaimed, "Iuka! What a name. Wonder where they got that, huh? I-oo-ka."

"Oh, dear God. We'll be hearing that for days." I peeled off my waterproof jacket and threw it in the back seat. Even on cooler days, it boiled me in my own juices, a zipped-and-velcroed sauna. I flung my arms over my head and let the wind fan wet patches. "Looks like nothing but fields ahead."

"That's another reason we found you, Andra." Mom's hands still wrenched in her lap, a nervous habit I inherited from her. "A maintenance crew stopped us. There's a pack of wild dogs about a mile ahead—four or so, they don't know—feeding on a deer carcass. When they tried to get the remains, one dog attacked them."

"I'm sure they'll be gone by the time I get there." I hoisted my backpack in place and stretched my calves while Dad spilled nuts everywhere.

Mom sighed, her frustration barometer. "Roy, you just had three scoops of ice cream. Stop eating those nuts. You're making a mess." She flicked her blue-grey eyes back to me. "Still, I think you should let us drive you through this part, Andra."

I repositioned my voodoo doll on my right shoulder, hoping to beat the impatient edge from my voice. "I can't cheat, Mom. I have to walk."

Mom shot from the driver's seat and bolted around the car. "Who made up these ridiculous rules?"

"I'm just trying to honor history—"

"That doesn't mean you should risk your life, Andra. Do you know how much I worry about you? Every mile of this.....this—"

"Stupid? Is that what you want to say?"

She slid a turquoise ring up and down her finger while Dad filled his face with more nuts. Nervous ticks defined every family moment. Rawness made us elemental.

I tightened the stays on my backpack and stepped away from her. "Believe me, I know how stupid this walk is. I have to get out here and do it every day, remember?" I stopped. To swat aggravation from my voice, I bit my lip and stretched my calves again. When I found calm, I continued. "I'm not doing anything people haven't done before me. I'll be fine."

"You always say that, but how do you know? I've gone along with this business for more than a week. I've watched cars almost hit you, and I've seen you crippled by pain. How can you possibly know those dogs won't go after you?"

"Because," I turned my face northward. "I have them to protect me."

"Who?"

I ignored her and walked away. She didn't like my voodoo doll mascot and questioned the voices I heard along the Trace. Dead pioneers. Ancient Native Americans. Soldiers and Spaniards and animals. Spirit walking, a friend called it. A notion that didn't jibe with Mom's devout faith, a faith I shared with her, though I made allowances for other mysteries, varied beliefs.

Because, at its heart, wasn't all faith the same explanation for things we couldn't see?

The closer I crept to the Meriwether Lewis site, the louder the voices grew. On sunny days, I heard them in my footsteps. They chattered in raindrops and rode the coattails of a gale.

One morning, they conjured a deer. It bounded up a hill and walked next to me. I saw its ears flick, heard its puffs of breath. Its hooves echoed on the highway, and it regarded me with one curious eye.

In the stillness, I heard voices. "We used to have these moments all the time. How do you people live without 'em?"

How did I?

Still, Mom was right to worry. When I walked onto an overpass, I didn't leave anything to chance. I carried one weapon. On my shoulder, next to my voodoo doll.

I never fired my police-issue mace, because I was afraid I'd aim the wrong way and spray myself in the face. Or the wind would carry the noxious mixture back at me. Panic always made me grasp the wrong things.

"I guess I'd better practice. Just in case." I yanked the canister from my shoulder and flipped its plastic top. When I pushed the red button, a stream of what looked like semen shot ten inches from its nozzle. I looked at its snout in disbelief. "That's all I get? One pathetic squirt of protec-tion? Somebody could have me in their trunk, halfway to who-knows-where, before this thing would help me." I almost hurled it into space. "Police-issue mace. I don't know why it doesn't come with a big, fat sign that reads 'Abduct Me'."

When I stopped shaking, I palmed the mace in my right hand, my thumb close to the red trigger. I followed the road until it bisected another field. "Surely this is the wild dog place." I scanned the muddy expanses on both sides. Though I wanted to run, I held steady. A rustle of trees was a possible attacker; a snort the hunger of insatiable hounds. "I wish I'd never read Edgar Allan Poe," I whispered as I marched into the open. The road was an elevated land bridge through broken fences. Plowed earth and scrub.

I telescoped my head from west to east, breath quickening with my heartbeat. Didn't hunters claim animals gave off more pheromones when they were spooked? And, once I allowed myself to think the word 'spooked,' I couldn't take it back.

I was a target.

For anything.

I galloped into a run, chanting, "I'm going to be fine. I'm going to be fine. I'm going to be fine. Step quick. Eyes on the horizon. Change sides of the road every twenty steps. Keep moving. Don't stop. I'm going to be fine. I am."

When I reached the trees, I slid underneath them and didn't look behind me. I loosened my grip on my mace and expected to find my palm print in plastic. Panting, I sat next to a milepost and slid my head between my knees.

Mom steered the car beyond me. When I stopped shaking, I snapped my milepost photo and walked to her open window.

Mom waited. Hands in her lap. Silent and still. "Those dogs were gone by the time we got there."

"Uh-huh. Looked that way." I fought to keep my voice even, furious she didn't come back to tell me.

"You remember my chiropractor?" My mother. The master of unexpected conversational tacks.

And how could I forget him? Mom saw him every week in my teens. For two years, she battled sciatica, while I wondered if she prolonged her visits because she

liked the way he hugged her. That's what she called his adjustments: Hugging her. She always noted how handsome he was.

"Yeah. I remember him."

"Well, he died last month. Mauled. By a pack of wild dogs." She prodded me with a perfect fingernail. "I worry about you, Andra. Always going on these hikes alone. Or with Michael. I'm afraid something like that'll happen to you."

As she drove up the highway, I squirted mace into her jet stream.

Did she make up that story about the dogs and the deer carcass to scare me into quitting?

It wouldn't be the first time.

CROSS ROAD BLUES
Robert Johnson

Andra was always into that theater stuff. I think she got the acting bug from me.

And her storytelling.

And her looks, most of 'em.

I remember her getting the lead in 'South Pacific' in college. I didn't want her to stay home for school. That was Linda's idea. I thought she needed to go away from home, build her own independence. Like I did. But when I got Andra into the University of Georgia, my alma mater, Linda had a fit.

"Andra Watkins is not going to that . . . . . . that den of iniquity." Linda's nostrils flared when she was mad, but I was pretty riled up, too.

"I went to that den of iniquity, and I turned out all right."

But nothing I said changed that woman's mind. Andra enrolled in the local college and kept doing plays. I was there, the day she came home and found Linda on the pot.

"Mom!" She breezed by my recliner and headed down the hallway. "My theater professor wants me to audition for the musical theater program at Florida State." I sat forward in my chair and listened. "He knows people there, and he thinks I'm good enough to win a place and transfer."

I could just see Linda there on her throne, that application straining in her hands. I expected her to use it to wipe

her butt. Her voice wafted down the hall, and I turned down the TV to catch it. "You're not majoring in musical theater, Andra."

"Why not? I've always loved it, and—"

"You're just not." A spigot ran. Probably Linda washing germs from that paper off her hands. She was so mad I could hear her over the flush of the toilet. "You need to major in something that you can do part-time when you have children—"

"I don't want to have children."

I chuckled. My daughter. Always digging in for a fight.

"Oh, you think that now, but you're young. You'll change your mind."

Their voices came toward me, and I sat back in my recliner. Didn't want 'em to know I was listening. When Linda made up her mind about something, it was just easier to take her side.

I never dreamed I'd spend my whole life stuck between two women. My mother and my wife. My wife and my daughter.

Andra trailed Linda into the den, still fighting. "I've always dreamed of performing, Mom. You know that."

"Dreaming only gets us in trouble."

I cranked up CNN, but I couldn't stop thinking about dreams. When I was Andra's age, I had 'em, too. Get outta Tennessee. Travel in the Army. Go to college and make my mother proud. I avoided women 'til I was thirty. Then I done gone and lost my mind. Married Linda. Started a family.

It wasn't that life didn't play out like my dreams. I just wanted more than going to work. Coming home. Breaking my back to provide for people who depended on me. I was always afraid of disappointing 'em, letting 'em down.

Being like my dad was.

People go into parenthood saying, "I won't do. I won't do. I won't do." But, at some point, they look back and realize they've become the very people they  *said they wouldn't be. Oh, I didn't drink. Didn't run around on Linda. Nothing like that.*

But I never knew how to talk to my children, like my father never knew what to say to me. I dreamed of being different, of having one of them close father-daughter rela-

tionships. *After trying all through Andra's teens, I knew I missed my window. I'd never live that dream.*

ONE STEP UP

Bruce Springsteen

Alabama wind. It blasted from the northwest and swirled the length of my body. Cars zipped past me, and I wondered if I looked like the Tasmanian devil from old Bugs Bunny cartoons, a funnel cloud with arms and legs. I dodged a path of wild dogs to stagger through endless fields, borders defined by scattered trees, a starker landscape than Mississippi.

My legs followed the will of unseen forces. Every step landed somewhere other than I intended.

"Four more miles to go!" I shouted but couldn't hear myself. Words were sucked into the ether around milepost 326. I shook my fist at the sky, and Nature crept in and almost stole my hat. With both hands gripping the brim, I forgot my resolve to find joy every day. Instead, I leaned back and bawled, "A wind tunnel? What else are you going to do to me?"

Was it my imagination, or did the Wind laugh?

Across the road, a tractor wove trenches in a field, spreading clouds of red dirt that crashed across the highway, an opaque wall of filth. I jumped up and down, shouted and waved, hoping he would stop to let me pass. I even considered mooning or flashing, because in that moment, I understood how some people did anything for a break.

Back and forth, machinery carved into land. I couldn't compete with the hum of the engine, the roar of

the gale. Defeated, I stumbled through dirty air and almost fell in the path of a minivan. It careened toward me, fighting the weather, and I moved into the ditch to avoid it. When I raised my arm to wave, howling forces snapped it backward at the elbow.

The van streaked into the grass and stopped next to me.

"I'm okay!" I started talking as soon as the passenger rolled down her window, but I caught myself when she wagged a paper rectangle in my face. Black lines. White letters.

My book.

"We came out here to meet you, and we need you to sign this."

Unthinkable requests were tricks of the wind. I leaned closer and cupped my hat brim next to my ears.

"What?"

"Our book! Your dad sold us one of your books back there at Colbert Ferry, and we want you to sign it."

A gust blew me into the door. I sneaked my eyes downward, hoping I didn't scratch it. The woman smiled and pressed the book flat, while the driver handed me a pen. "We're related to William Clark," he said.

"Through the Austins," a man chimed from the back seat.

"So when your dad told us you'd written a book about Meriwether Lewis, it wasn't a hard sell."

I leaned through the opening, a respite from the growl in my ears. "Where are you from?"

"Just up the road in Tennessee. We think what you're doing is incredible, walking the Trace and all. And writing about Meriwether Lewis."

"Incredible. Or incredibly crazy." I smiled at the three of them.

"Well, those historians think Lewis was crazy, but Clark's family, we all believe he was murdered."

My swollen fingers battled to scratch my name on the front page, but I didn't feel pain. Whenever I needed a lift, the Trace found a way. "I hope you like what I did with his story. It's kinda scary, knowing people who still care will read it and have opinions."

"We're looking forward to it."

I handed them a bent business card. "I hope you'll keep in touch. Thanks for coming out in this weather. You made my whole week."

As I peeled myself from the van, I forgot the wind. I covered the two miles to the Tennessee River in less than thirty minutes. My feet hovered above the ground. I weaved along the entrance road to Colbert Ferry and climbed into my parents' car for a late lunch.

Dad was talking before I touched my sandwich.

"Those people find you? Get you to sign their book?"

"Yes, Dad." I bit into smashed peanut butter and bread.

"You need to sign more of them books, Andra. I can't sell 'em if they ain't signed. People want 'em signed."

"Can I eat first, Dad?"

"Just don't get out of the car without signing them books."

My fingers were the size of bratwursts, and they trembled when I gripped my sandwich and forced it to my mouth. The inside of the car bounced like I floated on the open sea. I blinked, but the motion intensified. "I think I went too long today without eating."

Mom glanced in the rearview mirror. "Did you not stop for a snack?"

"I never found a sheltered place. Couldn't sit in the open, with all this wind." I fanned my face with my balloon-ish hand. "I'm a little dizzy. It'll pass."

Dad tapped the dashboard with his Georgia ring. "You better sign those books."

"Dad—"

"Roy—"

Mom and I blurted in stereo.

"Can I please eat and rest a few minutes without you nagging me, Dad?"

"I'm helping you. That's what I'm doing. This is your dream, but you ain't doing your part."

I could almost hear his speech to thirteen-year-old me. "Don't grow up to be a failure, Andra. You need to

learn to stick to the things you start. Have some stick-to-it-ive-ness about you."

I flung my uneaten sandwich across the back seat. "Dammit!" Mom plugged her ears with spangled fingers, but I didn't care if I offended her. Cardboard sawed my flesh as I opened a fresh box of books and scribbled my name. "Here. I'm signing them. Ten of them. You'd better sell every last one of these today."

"I already sold—"

"I don't care what you already sold, Dad. You've got two miles left. If I have to sign these in the shape I'm in, you have to sell them."

"But—"

"What's the matter? I bet you can't get rid of half these books in an hour."

"Watch me." Dad flicked the visor and grinned. Verbal sparring was his lifeline to me.

But when I opened the door and faced hurricane-like gusts, I saw my resolve fly away. I still had one significant landmark to cross. The John Coffee Memorial Bridge. The longest bridge on the Natchez Trace, its two lanes straddled the Tennessee River.

"Mom, I've got a bridge coming up. If we drive down to the landing, I'll scope it out first. You know, before I walk it. I'm not sure I should be on foot in this wind."

"I don't think you should," Dad muttered.

I squeezed his shoulder and fought to mask a laugh. "I don't care what you think, Dad."

"Heh-heh. I know."

Mom wound the car through the site and parked on a bluff. The Tennessee River churned like a pot boiling over.

Colbert Ferry got its name from the man-and-boat that moved people, animals and things back and forth across the river. In the aftermath of the Battle of New Orleans, the ferryman earned infamy by charging Andrew Jackson $50,000 to haul troops and materiel from one bank to the other. I eyed the rock-strewn gorge where the Old Trace met the water's edge. If Meriwether Lewis traveled that far south, he crossed the river there. Maybe he stood where I did, awaiting the ferry.

I imagined his day. Illness forced him from the Mississippi River at Memphis. He recuperated at Fort Pickering for two weeks before embarking upon an overland journey with Chickasaw Indian agent James Neely and two servants. Neely was headed as far as Nashville. He offered to escort the ailing Lewis and help him find another travel companion.

They drank their way through the backcountry and lost a valuable horse. According to Neely, Lewis ordered him to find it, while he pressed onward to Grinder's Stand.

Windblown voices smacked my face. "Have you been listening, girl? We couldn't walk on water. We were all ferried across."

I looked around the empty parking lot. Mom and Dad waved from the Mercury, engine running.

A car would be my ferry.

When I settled in the back seat, the wind still roared in my head. "Drive me across the bridge, Mom."

Dad fastened his seat belt. "That's the first sensible thing you've said on this entire trip, Andra."

"You just figure out how to sell ten books in two miles, Old Man." I leaned into the leather headrest and closed my eyes.

Two miles to go. Another 114 miles to the end.

Would I ever cross the finish line?

Not Without My Father

FOLLOW YOU, FOLLOW ME
Genesis

Collinwood, Tennessee. Population 991.

"Here's the room, Hon." I limped through a commercial glass door and followed another Linda into an oblong room. Two beds shared the same space. Fluorescent lighting dotted ceiling tile. "The bathroom is so small, because we planned it as an office initially. But with all the bicyclists on the Trace and whatnot, we converted it into places to stay."

When I closed the door, I couldn't turn around in the bathroom. I inspected the minuscule shower and wondered whether Dad would fit.

But a bed was a bed, and I needed a bed. And a welcoming soul.

I opened the bathroom door and smiled at the Other Linda. "It's perfect."

With a bed three feet from me, I didn't care where I stayed. The place was clean. The main room was spacious, and the Other Linda was attentive and helpful. After fifteen miles of wind and rain and more wind, I wanted to collapse.

Mom interrupted my bed-ward trajectory. "We were really hoping for a bathtub. She needs to soak her feet."

"Mom, I don't—"

Mom put one manicured hand on a hip. "Show her your feet, Andra."

"No. Really. Nobody needs to see my feet. Nobody."

Still, I fiddled with my laces, ready to play.

"You can come upstairs and use my tub." The Other Linda scooted to the door at the sight of one crusty sock. "I'll get it ready. You don't even have to knock. You just come on in." She was gone before we could argue.

Mom's face glowed with victory. "I don't know how you did fifteen miles today. You look like you're about to fall over. You go ahead. I'll bring our stuff in."

"Isn't Dad going to help?" I winced as I peeled sock-and-skin from my other foot.

"No. I dropped him on Main Street. He mumbled something about five books to sell."

"He'll never do it."

I left her to unload and dragged myself up outdoor stairs to the owners' suite.

The Other Linda met me at the door. "My grandchildren's with me, so you lock yourself in. The five-year-old might surprise you if you don't. I got everything ready, Hon."

I followed her through a bedroom to her master bath. While I waited for epsom salts to dissolve, I held the counter and tugged my clothes. Undressing was never easy when I couldn't bend my legs. I inched compression pants down my thighs and wondered how I didn't fall and crack my skull.

Strength seeped through pain. The Tennessee River buffeted me, but its waves applauded. I was almost through my second state of three, territory Meriwether Lewis touched. Agony couldn't obliterate my pride at seeing my father keep going, at knowing I shared an unusual gift. An adventure with my aging parents.

 I sank into scalding water and picked bandage adhesive from my feet. One toenail clung to a web of dead skin. Two toes glowed purple. Remnants of dark nail polish mimicked gangrene. I rolled my eyes and murmured, "My feet will never be the same."

Fifteen minutes. Thirty. I leaned into steam and

soaked until the water cooled, my longest bath since the jacuzzi in Raymond, Mississippi. I swabbed out the bath and returned to my room, hoping the Other Linda didn't think me tacky for staying an hour.

Because Dad wasn't lurking outside, always needing to pee.

I missed him. I didn't realize how I'd grown accustomed to his toilet urges until he wasn't there to interrupt. Dad blew through our room's glass door before sleep claimed me. "Hey, Andra. An-dra! You asleep? Hey! You sleeping?" He poked my arm. Once. Twice.

Opening my eyes hurt. "Not anymore, Dad."

"Well, I done sold ten books. Ten. To that coffee shop up the street."

"You bribed them. Or gave them away for free."

"No, I did not. You bet me I couldn't sell five books before the end of today, and I done sold ten. Double."

"Okay. Great." I sank into satin sheets and covered my face with a pillow.

Dad lorded over me, jabbing his finger into my shield. "There's a catch, though."

"What?"

"They want 'em wholesale. Discounted, 'cause they're gonna sell 'em in their store. What'll you sell 'em for?"

His finger almost gouged my eye when I bolted upright. "They don't count! You can't claim to sell ten books and discount them!"

"Ten books is ten books. You didn't define how I had to do it. Just that I had to sell 'em before the end of the day. And the coffee shop wants to buy 'em, for a wholesale price." He crossed his arms over his bulge of belly, his eyes glittering. The man never stopped pushing me.

I threw my pillow across the room and hit Mom coming in the door, but I continued my rant. "Fine. You sell them for this price, and not one penny less. And if they won't agree to that, then you lost our bet."

Dad wagged his finger in my face. "You're buying my dinner tonight, and I'm powerful hungry." The door slapped his behind on his way out.

I looked at Mom. "He's walking all the way over there? Seriously? It's almost four blocks to the coffee shop. This is what I have to do to get that fat man to exercise?"

"Let me get you some dinner before he gets back." She handed me a menu for the local diner, one of Collinwood's only eating establishments. My stomach rumbled as I scanned two pages of fried carbs. Almost 350 miles walked, and I wasn't down a single pound. My mouth watered at the description of their homemade burger, but I kept my eyes trained to the salad section, never a good choice when the specialty was deep fried goodness.

I tossed the menu aside. "I'm not hungry."

"You've got to eat, Andra. You barely ate lunch." Mom forced the plastic-coated pages between my fingers.

"That was Dad's fault."

"No, you both enjoy sparring."

I dropped the menu and pulled the bedspread over my head. Mom's voice penetrated my cocoon. "I'm going to get you a hamburger. Roy'll be up at that place for at least an hour, sussing out new strangers to talk to. You can eat your dinner and pretend to be asleep when he tries to claim his prize."

Bedding vaulted everywhere when I sat up. "How am I gonna sleep, when the whole sleep apnea machine business'll be gurgling feet from my bed?"

"I don't know how you're going to sleep, but I know I'm sleeping with you. Three nights of sharing a bed with him is plenty."

Before I could argue, she darted through the front door. I ran my fingers along the arches of my shredded feet. Every bloody gash was a personal victory. "Only a few more days, Andra. Exactly a week. You never thought you'd get this far."

Dad strutted into the room waving a check. "I sold 'em. Ten books." He threw the check onto the bedspread. "I won our bet. Now, aren't you gonna buy your dear old dad some fried onion rings?"

"Mom's over at the diner, getting my supper. You go over there and tell her to buy whatever you want." Before he made it through the door, I yelled, "But if you eat a whole order of onion rings, you'd better not stink up this room all night!"

Not Without My Father

I WALK THE LINE
Johnny Cash

Two days later, I stood on the brink of another fifteen miles and wondered what five hours walking uphill would do to hamstrings and desiccated feet. When I tightened my laces at milepost 360, I distracted myself with the sound of falling water. A rocky creek burbled through a chasm next to the highway, soothing company through my first two miles.

By the time I made the restroom facility at Glenrock Branch, my legs and feet warmed to my will. I used a real toilet and jogged down a steep path to the creek. If I stretched, I could dip my toes into rushing water, still icy at the tail end of winter. After a few minutes, I couldn't feel anything below my ankles. For the first time in almost a month, I numbed both feet at once.

I almost had an orgasm.

"Andra! You okay?" Dad's gut strained over the fence bordering the parking lot.

"I'm great, Dad! Just making a video in front of this rock formation." I waved my iPhone in his direction. The creek powered around a natural rock cairn. It teetered over my head, stacked by a giant hand.

Dad took a couple of steps down the incline. Just two, lest he exert himself in the reverse climb. He waited for me to join him. Before I was halfway, he was talking.

"You know there's a big hill coming up."

"Don't tell me. Don't tell me. Don't tell me!" I panted next to him. "I don't look at the map for anything other than a bathroom or a place in the book, Dad. You know that."

"But we done drove it, and it's mighty steep."

I pulled my hat over my ears. "I told you I don't want to know what's coming."

"And crooked."

"Dad—"

"Cars probably won't be able to see you on them curves." He twisted his black Georgia Bulldog hat and looked at his feet. "I, uh........I just want you to be careful."

I touched his arm and tried to keep my voice even. "I'll walk on the shoulder."

"Ain't no shoulder. That's what I'm saying." He shrugged away from me. "One side of the road's a sheer wall of rock, with a big drop off to this here creek on the other. You gotta climb it on the highway, and drivers, if they're going fast and all, well, they might not see you."

I remembered the time I rode a school friend's moped. He took me for a fifteen-year-old joyride. I didn't ask my parents. I just hopped on. We putted along neighborhood streets. Even found a few piles of dirt to jump for an elevated heartbeat.

When I got home, Dad sat stone faced in his recliner.

"Get to your room, Andra. I'm giving you a spanking." He already had his belt stretched taut in his hands.

"Why? What did I do?" I couldn't remember the last time my parents spanked me. Corporal punishment was a faint memory from elementary school.

He waved the belt inches from my face. "Do you know what I saw from them motor bikes when I worked at that funeral home at the University of Georgia? Mangled-up bodies? Girls I couldn't even tell was girls? I had to scrape one of 'em off the highway. In pieces. Didn't know if it was a person or roadkill."

Tears filmed his eyes. I couldn't ignore the strength of his memories, the manifestation of his pain. "I didn't know, Dad. You never told me."

"Well, I just did." He fiddled with his belt clasp and wouldn't look at me.

"Dad." I slipped my arm around his broad shoulder. "I didn't know riding a moped would upset you like that. Please don't punish me for your memories. If it's that big a deal, I won't do it again, okay?"

It took him almost three more decades to admit he feared seeing his daughter turned into shredded meat.

I jiggled the circa-1980 hearing aid perched above a hairy ear. "At least, I'll be able to hear them coming. I love you, too, Dad." Before he responded, I trotted toward the road.

Maybe we were both growing.

The Trace took a right turn and followed a cliff. My knuckles scraped wet rock layers as I charged up the slope, determined my will would make it easy.

From Natchez to Nashville, I gained almost a thousand feet of elevation. Spread over 444 miles, I thought I wouldn't feel the incline. It was only when a reader asked about actual elevation changes that I looked online. Serious climbing would happen in Tennessee.

By the next bend, I cursed Achilles and his stupid heel. Pavement merged with sky along a ten percent grade. Tight ankles refused to stretch downward, forcing me to charge the slope on tiptoe. Oozing blisters were my sole grip on the roadway. My determination fled as the novelty of rolling hills and picturesque creeks was replaced with wheezing and grinding teeth.

"I know I read it, but I didn't think I'd have to do it all at once." I swiped my sweaty face on my sleeve and blinked to refocus. Falling water. Newborn red buds. A woodpecker zooming back and forth ahead of me. It tapped a tree trunk, and I imagined Morse code. "You can do it. You can do it. You can."

As I took a clearer step, a car blasted around the curve, thirty feet from me. I rolled along the shoulder to avoid being hit and smacked into a ragged rock wall. Burning oil clogged my nostrils. I examined knuckles, elbows, knees. "I can't believe I didn't take off several layers of skin." I heaved my right foot onto empty pavement and ignored the stitch in my back. The car never braked.

I hauled myself to a plateau. Rocky outcrops gave way to graceful fields and fenced pastures. I tried to skip along the grassy shoulder. Beauty over pain. Adventure over agony. Two trees squeaked together, a melody I didn't notice in the snarl of everyday life. I snapped a picture with my foot on milepost 370.

"This is probably the last day I'm going to walk alone."

Acknowledgement gutted me. In spite of the challenges, I found joy in walking alone. Just my broken body. The rolling movie reel of Nature. And my thoughts. My soul bled remorse on an empty hornets nest, into the spiky balls of a gum tree. I squeaked through a drenched field, and I stood amid thousands of daffodils.

I spread my arms and twirled, startled by the realization that I didn't want to finish. My walk was magical, mythic joy. Even at its hardest, the Natchez Trace rewarded me. Tears ran through the dirt on my cheeks. "I'm gonna miss this Life when it's over."

A car slowed as it approached me, and before I could wave, the passenger flashed green and white through the open window. I threw both hands over my head, thumbs up. "My book! You're reading my book!" I danced with daffodils long after engine noise faded.

I almost forgot about my book. I risked my life to convince people to try my novel, because I thought if I demonstrated dedication to my story, a few more people might read it.

I no longer cared.

Countless layers of blistered skin slathered off selfish motives. My walk was about more than pages, bound in colored paper. I never understood the value of an adventure with my aging parents. Civilizations repeat the mistakes of history, much like families replicate dysfunctional dynamics, generation after generation. Walking almost 444 miles stripped away expectations and knit me to Mom and Dad. We would leave a storied place and rewrite history.

Milepost 373 wobbled into sight. I peeled off my hat. My scalp tingled when I ran fingers through my hair. I blinked several times, but the world still tilted. "Two more miles. Damn. I was so busy being in the moment, I think I forgot to eat."

My phone lit up before I could summon Mom. I slid my finger along the screen. "Mom? Where are you?"

"On a side road, just down from milepost 374."

"Good. Wait there. I'm dizzy."

"I can come and get you if you're—"

"No." My teeth ripped into a protein bar. "Time got away from me, and I didn't eat. I'm gonna sit with you and Dad and eat my lunch, okay?"

Dad's voice was background static. "Maybe I can hold it 'til she's through."

"Not having a place to go hasn't stopped you anywhere else, Roy. And Andra? I've got potato chips for you."

Potato chips. I was still shallow enough to find motivation in junk food. The promise of carbs righted my world's axis. "Tell Dad not to eat them all before I get there."

"He might, Andra. Better hurry."

Fifteen minutes later, I munched salty decadence in my parents' back seat and computed a total step estimate on my iPhone's calculator. By the time I walked into Nashville, my feet would've carried me over one million thirteen thousand steps, almost all on asphalt.

Backcountry hikers have the luxury, if one could call it that, of varied terrain. Ups and downs shift the impact of movement on muscles and joints, and different surfaces distribute the shock of each step. Climbing rocks and scrambling through steep ravines can ravage a body, much like any long walk will destroy the feet.

Repetitive motion injuries dogged my steps. A week from the finish, my knees locked up when I rested for more than fifteen minutes. Geography didn't matter. Bed. Shower. Car. I never forgot screaming legs or mauled feet.

Even with a positive focus and an intention to find joy every day, agony fucked me in a relentless gang-bang. I hoped it was better for agony than it was for me.

Before I started my walk of the Natchez Trace, I thought my feet would toughen up, grow accustomed to the abuse. But the gods of the Trace had other plans. Meriwether Lewis was its most famous victim, gone at thirty-five in a mysterious death that would remain unsolved for all time. Did all the faceless people who walked its length, year after year, ache like me?

Potato chips carried me through my last mile. I was lighter, somehow. I climbed in the car and directed Mom to our next stand: Buffalo River Farm and Studio Bed and Breakfast. We navigated a dirt road and stopped at a red outbuilding flanked by black cattle. Two labrador retrievers bounded around me as I sputtered from the car.

"Boys! Stop that." A woman materialized to shake my hand. I marveled at her mud-spattered cowboy boots and relaxed air. "I'm Donna Branch, the innkeeper. You must be Andra. And you must be pooped. Let's get you to your room."

I followed her through her art studio and into her sprawling inn. Relaxed music wafted from a TV area made for Dad. She stopped in the gleaming chef's kitchen. "Here's the Keurig. Help yourself to anything. And your rooms are around the corner. Just there. I've already turned down your bed, and your towels are next to the shower."

I wanted to kiss her.

Ten minutes later, no one could drag me from bed. Anticipation was  another variation on pain, perhaps more excruciating than the physical. My body always did things my mind doubted. Growth happened when I overcame my mind.

The ceiling fan whirred as I considered my next day. Mileposts 375 to 390 included the one hallowed spot

I undertook the whole walk to visit. To kneel at the marker of a man whose death was deemed unsolvable.

Meriwether Lewis never married, though he had ample opportunity to become a father on his Western expedition. While he and his men screwed their way through the West, modern scientists discovered no link to Lewis progeny.

His expedition journals spanned volumes. Yet, he was still a mystery.

Did he suffer from malaria, bi-polar disorder, alcoholism, venereal disease or a combination of crippling ailments? If he was often unhinged, as some historians claimed, how did his men spend almost three years in his company and fail to record it? Why were they willing to follow him anywhere, even if he was the only person who believed his way was right? How could he abuse his body for thousands of miles and survive, only to die on the Natchez Trace?

My walk didn't answer those questions any more than I knew how Dad processed his father's lifetime alcoholism. I wasn't born when his mother drowned in a sea of congestive heart failure. Grainy pictures were my only record of his days in the United States Army.

To Dad, everything was a story. Stories were his shields. I sifted through words to piece together who Dad was. Where he came from. How he grew into the man who fathered me. For the first time, I understood the plight of historians who interpreted nuggets of Meriwether Lewis's life. We sift truth from what we're given.

I sat up on the bed and rubbed lotion into my cramping calves, but action didn't hit the pause button on my mind.

If Dad told me who he was through his stories, why did I question it? When he was gone, would I be able to explain who he was? Or, like Meriwether Lewis, would I only hold a few bits of a thousand-part puzzle?

I strained to hear over the television. Dad was in the common area, watching sports instead of the latest conjectures about the missing Malaysian airliner. Donna was fresh meat for stories I'd heard for decades. She brewed Dad a cup of coffee he'd hold in his hands but wouldn't

drink. He told her he grew up with cows grazing in fields just like hers. Did I hear tears when he told the story of how his family's land was flooded by the TVA? I almost called him a liar during his speech about avoiding sugar because of diabetes, but he outed himself when he accepted an overflowing bowl of ice cream and cookies.

I listened for new nuggets, for fresh clues to Dad's identity.

When he shambled outside to stare at the cows, I dragged myself into the kitchen and found Donna at the French doors, watching him. I punched the button on the coffeemaker. "I'm sorry. Dad'll talk your head off." Hazelnut caffeine streamed from the Keurig, a nutty scent that made me swoon. "He never met a stranger, even though he feels like a stranger to me."

Donna kept her eyes trained on the windows. "He's my dad made over. I lost him last year, and you know what? Listening to your dad talk is like having my dad back for a little while." Her cowboy boots scraped through the sliding door to her studio, where she made glass-bound books with coptic binding. Before the door closed, she whispered, "Thank you for bringing him to stay."

THE GOLDEN AGE
Beck

Them cows. Buffalo River in the distance. I sat on that porch and breathed the scent of my Tennessee childhood. 'Til that moment, I didn't know it was possible to travel back in time. To feel like a boy in the body of an eighty-year-old man.

But I did it.

I sat there and heard my dead father's voice. Relived the only story I didn't want my daughter to know.

We was working in the cow pasture along a creek that fed into the Ocoee River. Cutting burrs off the bank. Me. My daddy. And my future brother-in-law. I reckon I was about six years old.

Cows charged around us most of the day. 'Bout scared me to death, but I kept working. Them burrs cut into my hands and stuck to my clothes, but I didn't let Dad know I was hurting. He'd only laugh and call me a sissy-boy.

I hope I never made my children feel thataway.

Around eleven in the morning, the sun was beating down on us. Must've been right near a hundred degrees. I threw my sickle in the mud and told Dad I was going up to the house, 'cause I knew Momma'd have a tall glass of lemonade for her miracle boy.

I took off, not even bothering to avoid them cow patties everyplace. But before I could make the bridge, Dad shouted, "Don't let the troll under that bridge get you, Roy Lee."

Well, I didn't want him to know it, but I was scared of that troll. I heard stuff under there and thought I saw shriveled-up bodies all around Dad's property. It was why I didn't mind working next to him, in spite of his drinking all day.

A drunk was better than no defender.

Before I knew what I was doing, I wheeled on my heels and ran at him, flailing with bloody fists, while he pushed me back with a hand on my forehand and laughed and laughed.

"You goddamn sonofabitch!" I screamed through his cackles. "Don't you tell me about no goddamn troll! You can go straight to hell, you sonofabitch!"

Dad held me 'til I exhausted myself. I fell into a pile of them burrs while he took out his flask and helped himself to another swig of moonshine. "Want some, Roy Lee?"

I grabbed it outta his hands and swallowed a gulp of fire or several.

"You fight them trolls like that, and they won't bother you no more." Dad slipped his flask in his shirt pocket and started hacking at the creek bank.

I could almost smell his sweat, could see him just beyond the trees at the edge of Donna's property.

I wanted to tell Andra she was fighting them trolls, and she was winning.

Instead, I sat there on that porch. And I watched my father until he faded out of sight.

WALKING TO YOU

Everything But the Girl

After a biscuit-and-bacon-filled breakfast, Mom and Dad prepared to leave me at milepost 375. "We're going back to Collinwood to get your compression pants, Andra."

I forgot one of my two pairs of compression tights. As a woman of a certain age, I wore them under my hiking pants for extra support. And for vanity.

Mostly for vanity. I didn't want to end my walk with varicose veins.

I hiked away from the Buffalo River Valley, ready to meet Meriwether Lewis. He awaited me at milepost 386.9. A pile of granite and a broken shaft in a pioneer cemetery. I stood at his grave two years before, and I promised I'd weave him a new story. If his nickel wasn't a message, going back to his resting place might reveal what he really thought.

If dead people think.

I hauled myself to an overlook and sat in the sun. As I swung my legs, I wondered what the view was like when Lewis rode there. The vivid green of spring implied Life. Hope. Even rebirth. When Lewis traveled in October, dead leaves were morbid confetti. Was he thinking about Death as he crept toward his own?

Thirty minutes later, I rejoined the Parkway. No one would ever know what Lewis contemplated in the hours before he died. I procrastinated because seeing his grave

would mark the emotional end of my walk.

I wasn't ready to move on.

As I processed that admission, I looked up and saw my parents' Mercury Grand Marquis, parked in the high-way, passenger door open. I ran. "Mom! Dad! Is that you? Are you all right?" When I reached the empty car, I steered it onto the shoulder and shut off the engine. Mom's purse gaped on the seat beside an empty sleeve of sugar-free cookies. I grabbed the keys and locked the doors. "Dad!!!" I leaned back and roared. "Daddy, help me find you!"

Plaid flashed through trees. I pounded down a slope and closed the gap between Dad and me. But I almost tripped over my feet. My father stood there, barely concealed by bushes and weeds. His pants were around his ankles, and mountains of soiled toilet paper surrounded him. He didn't hear me as he scrubbed excrement from his suspenders, but it didn't matter, because it was everywhere. It speckled his khakis and sprayed along the back of his shirt.

The sins of the daughters, visited upon the fathers.

I tried to scoot away, to pretend I never saw him, but he ruined my escape.

"Andra! I......uh......."

My mouth moved, but I struggled to force something through it.

Mom came up behind me. "Oh, Roy. When you said you needed to stop, I thought you meant number one."

Dad threw another wad of toilet paper on the ground and ran his eyes along the highway. "Golly, I'm glad they's nobody around."

"I'm gonna have to take you back to the B and B to clean yourself up." She turned toward the car, and I followed. "I wonder whether there's a big piece of plastic in the trunk."

I stepped in her path, scorched her with furious eyes. "Why didn't you tell me Dad was this bad, Mom?"

"He didn't want you to know."

"And that's a reason not to tell a child her dad is—"

"You're not a child, Andra."

"Fine, Mom. You're right. As an adult, I have a right to know about my parents' health. How often does Dad have accidents like this?"

She became fascinated with the paint on her toenails.

"How many, Mom?"

"Oh, not much."

"Why do you always talk in approximations? Daily? A couple a week? What?"

"Well, it depends, Andra. Most of the time, he makes it to the bathroom before it starts."

"So—"

"Twice on the Trace, but we were able to take care of it before we picked you up."

I reeled for guilting my father into taking a road trip when he should've stayed home. For being too consumed with my own agenda to notice his decline. "My God. He really shouldn't be here."

"He didn't care whether he should've, Andra. It only mattered that he was."

Dad barreled from the trees and shrugged us off as we tried to help him into the passenger seat. "You women are making too much of this. I'm all right. Same thing happened to you the other day, Andra."

Before I could frame a response, Mom gunned the engine and was gone.

Would I ever have another adventure with my father?

Another engine snapped me from my thoughts. I stepped from the path of a blue car and wagged my usual thumbs-up sign to motion them on.

But the car stopped. Its driver opened the passenger door. His flabby arms wore sleeves of paint, and he didn't smile.

"You need to get in."

I backed a couple of steps, beyond the range of his grasp. "No, I'm okay. I'm walking the Trace. I'll be fine."

"Come on. Get in. Let me give you a lift."

I couldn't make out his face behind the lumberjack

beard. Was he short or tall? Muscular or wimpy? My fingers crept toward my mace. "I don't need a ride. I already told you. I'm walking."

"I saw you walking around 320 down in Alabama. Seen you several other times. You really need to let me give you a ride." He leaned over the armrest and toggled the handle on the glove box.

"No. I don't." I stumbled into a run before I saw whatever weapon he might have.

His motor lurched behind me. I squeezed the mace and ran into the forest, weaving between weeds and tree trunks until I couldn't see the highway. While he gunned his engine, I gulped every oily exhale. Rough bark scraped my knuckles as I crouched behind a gum tree and pulled out my phone. My hands shook, but I fumbled with my lifeline. Listened for muffled footsteps. Rustling leaves and cracking limbs. When the screen finally lit, the upper-left hand corner read NO SERVICE.

I leaned my forehead into wood and stopped breathing. Since Jackson, Mississippi, no rangers crossed my path. Over 300 miles. A deadlocked Congress left me to fend for myself. I couldn't summon a ranger or hope for one to rescue me.

It wasn't the first time I wished for more funding for the forgotten Natchez Trace and its people.

Five minutes. Ten. Fifteen. Engine noise rattled the Trace, but it crescendoed and faded. I crept to the forest's edge and scanned the roadway.

The blue car was gone.

I staggered through a ravine and stopped at the road. Before I could check my signal, the phone vibrated in my hand.

> We're on our way. Where have you been?

My fingers tapped the screen in answer to Mom's text.

> I've been right here. All the time.

If they could hide Dad's deteriorating condition, I could shield them from worry.

It wasn't exactly a lie.

WALK ON THE WILD SIDE
Lou Reed

As I hot-footed it toward the Meriwether Lewis site, my phone chimed again. Visitors. Two people were careening down the Trace to meet me.

When I invited readers to join me on my Natchez Trace walk, I didn't think anyone would. Who would take time off to hike a neglected highway? With unpredictable weather and poisonous snakes and biting bugs? I buried an invitation in a blog post and forgot it.

Until I heard from Lisa Kramer, a writer and reader in Massachusetts. I found her online when she wrote about an Eastern European trip to study movement with gypsies. The more I read, the more I recognized myself. Theater. Writing. Supportive husbands. A yearning to travel. Even though our correspondence was online, I considered Lisa a dear friend.

But I never expected to open my email and read her message: "I'd really like to come walk with you."

Was she crazy? Maybe she'd show up, and we'd loathe each other on sight. What if she was bitten by a snake? Could she sue me? Convinced she was being nice, I turned my attention to my empty screen and typed, "You should. You totally should."

Once I hit Send, I forgot about Lisa.

The next morning, my inbox blinked with another email. From Lisa.

"I've been looking at flights. It's pretty expensive to

fly from Boston to Nashville."

Was she serious?

I did a quick Google search and found several discounted options. "You can afford it if you pick these dates." My psyche was drunk on the notion that one stranger wanted to take part. "Invite yourself to stay with Tori. She's in Nashville. At least you've met her. I'm staying with her at the end of my walk, and I don't even know her."

Tori Nelson was another person I met online. I started following her because she invited readers to plan her Very Bloggy Wedding. She solicited votes on dresses and makeup options. Even her bridal hairdo. For months, I expressed my opinions, marveling that I sort of knew someone whose balls were gigantic enough to cede her wedding to strangers. How could I not love all six feet of her on sight?

I couldn't believe it when Tori and Lisa pulled up next to me on the Natchez Trace. Whoops, shouts and music vibrated through trees. Like life-long friends, I hugged Lisa through an open window, not caring how I smelled. "I can't believe you're here!" I shouted as I Chinese-fire-drilled around the car to smother Tori with BO.

Lisa pushed a screwdriver curl from her face. "We made it happen!"

They planned to walk the last four miles of my day. A rendezvous at the Meriwether Lewis site. A picnic they prepared. When they motored up the highway, I wasn't alone anymore. They threw a wall of pink confetti, enough to repel any predator. I was dazzled by girl power glitter.

Until I thought about the road ahead.

For my whole trek, I carried specific images of my time at the Meriwether Lewis site. Walking alone along the abandoned road. I knew where to pick up the Old Trace, and I planned to follow his footsteps into the clearing where he died. I would walk across the ruins of Grinder's Stand  and cover the distance to Merry's monument in silence, my Lewis and Clark nickel cupped in my right hand. Alone, I would kiss the nickel and whisper a blessing, before placing it on Merry's grave.

Maybe he would even whisper, "Thank you."

I looked at the pink noise maker in my hand and feared Lisa and Tori would think my plodding production insane. I put aside the logistics of Merry's grave and dialed my mother. "Mom! Hi! How's Dad?"

She sighed. "He's talking to Donna again. You know him."

I heard myself say, "Well, I think you'd better come back this way. A guy just stopped and tried to get me into his car."

"Where are you?"

"Milepost 383."

"Don't move. We'll be there in ten minutes." Mom rang off before I could reassure her. My feminist protection squad was spreading its net along the Trace. Nobody would go after a woman with a cardboard party horn.

Eight minutes later, Mom and Dad rumbled through grass next to me. "You need to cut this day short," Dad talked from an open window. "You shouldn't be out here with some maniac. When I worked at that funeral home, I saw what people could do."

"I'm sure he's long gone by now, Dad."

"Still, it would make us feel better if we kept an eye on you.......just until you get to the Meriwether Lewis site and those girls join you." Mom raised the window and accelerated to the next bend before I could argue. When I got close, she pulled further ahead.

A half-mile from the entrance to the Meriwether Lewis site, they steered their car to the left and disappeared. I pumped a fist and celebrated. "Finally. I can find the trail Lewis took."

But when I crossed the highway to photograph the Meriwether Lewis sign, my dreams of walking to Lewis's grave shattered. The Mercury Grand Marquis blocked the entrance. Mom hopped out and opened the back door. "We'll drive you. This road's busy, plus we drove around the park. They're doing some forest work."

"Mom—"

"She thinks she saw a blue car," Dad interjected. "Plus, them girls is in there."

I slipped off my backpack and surrendered. "I'm sure

they'd love to know you call them girls, Dad."

"Well? Ain't you? Girls? I mean, Linda here's a girl, and you're a—"

"Okay, Dad."

"And that Charlayne Hunter, she was a girl. First African-American woman at the University of Georgia. You're tough as she was. Different kind of tough, walking all this way."

I swiped my eyes and settled into the back seat. Dad complimented me three times on my tri-state hike. I couldn't process his praise.

Yet.

FAST CAR

Tracy Chapman

When I was at UGA, I lived in a funeral home attic. Worked there, too, for room and board. While everybody else went on dates and got drunk, I drove the hearse out country roads in the middle of the night. Scraping body parts off the highway. Even got to embalm people from time to time.

And everything.

One night, we was up at the funeral home and in came a call. Late. Two African-Americans had been admitted to the University of Georgia. Forced desegregation, they called it. We walked between classes wondering what was gonna happen when the lights went out. Well, we didn't have to wonder long.

That night, there was a big basketball game. Georgia playing Georgia Tech was always tense. All hell broke loose when Georgia Tech won in overtime. People was smashing bottles and throwing bricks and generally causing a ruckus.

But some of them thought they could vent their spleens about race. People joined the mob, and it spread all over campus. Broken windows. Fires.

We got the call because most small-town funeral homes used their hearses as ambulances in those days. Just in case somebody became a customer.

By the time we got there, they'd called in the police. Tear gas was so thick you couldn't cut it. We got the body board outta the back and picked our way past Dean Tate. I'll never forget his bald head and booming voice as he yanked IDs and expelled person after person. Don't know why he thought

expelling 'em was gonna make 'em stop. A Georgia institution, that man was.

Anyway, we got inside the girls' dorm and found the room where that Charlayne Hunter was holed up. When we elbowed in there, she was passed out on the bed, her face covered in wet towels. I don't even think she knew we was moving her, but we strapped her on the body board and took her to the hearse without getting beaned with a brick or cut open by glass.

I really thought that'd be my last night. I was afraid to go in there, but I was even more scared of how I'd live with myself if I didn't. If something happened to that girl, I'd have never forgiven myself.

I saw her on campus after that, but I never told her I was one of the guys who got her out. Didn't think she'd want to relive that night or know anybody saw her thataway. But I still wished I could see her, tell her how much I admire what she done. She probably lived every day wondering when her being there was gonna start another riot, not knowing if she'd survive 'til graduation. Those college years had to be a lonely walk.

I was glad I could be there to help her take a few steps in the right direction. She's gone on to have a pretty amazing life.

And that never surprised me. When I moved them towels that night and saw the look on her face, I knew she'd beat anything.

My daughter's got that look, too.

WALK AND DON'T LOOK BACK
Temptations

As I giggled with Lisa and Tori, I fought to maintain my public face. Through helpings of barbecue chicken wings and hummus, I kept one eye on my father.

He sat on a bench. Alone. His hearing aids were probably muted against three grown women cackling like teenagers, but his face was cracked and uneven. Void of stories. Even flat. I scrolled my eyes from him to Mom and wondered whether he was really okay. Into my fifth week with him, I knew he drew from a dwindling well of strength.

While Tori fed chicken to a stray dog, Lisa tried to engage Dad. She twirled over a granite compass. Meriwether Lewis's profile lit up its coordinates, a directional map of his achievements. "We knew you were Andra's father before we met you."

"How'd you know me?" Dad rested his arms on his belly.

"You were in the park shop. Selling books." Lisa's theatrical gestures were sweeping. Sincere. Her limbs remembered the grace of the gypsies. "We came in, trying to convince them to carry Andra's book."

"Yeah. But we saw Andra's famous book-selling Dad, and we knew we were bested." Tori sat cross-legged on the ground and waved potato chips at the hungry dog. She stretched her long legs. Her eyes shone with the confidence of a towering woman who'd wear a beehive as her

wedding hairdo. "Maybe I outta take this dog home with me. Do you think I should? I think I should."

"You should." I bit into a cold biscuit stuffed with bacon.

The bench creaked when Dad leaned forward. "Course I sell better'n you.......what's your name again?"

"Lisa. Absolutely. Andra'll never find a better salesman than you."

Lisa stuffed a pita chip with hummus, and Tori teased the dog with another chicken bone. We were a comfortable threesome. I admired Lisa's earnest tenacity as much as I loved Tori's self-deprecating hilarity.

I elevated my feet on the bench and studied Dad. He always wanted to be somebody. Foiled ambition was the reason he almost left us in my teens. Everyone encounters a moment in Life when they realize they're running out of Time.

I hoped I gave him Time. Through telling his stories, he was the character he always longed to be. With little girl notions, I still believed he could do anything.

I sat next to Mom. "Of course you're better than them, Dad. You're the best."

He bellowed his first big laugh.

In my imaginings of the Meriwether Lewis site, I never heard Dad's laughter. Or my own. I discarded my reverent plans and charged into the cemetery with two new friends. They made jokes while I found the right spot for my nickel. "Okay, let's create this scene." Lisa, the theater director, assigned our roles. I climbed Tori's six-feet to her back, while Lisa crawled between her legs.

"Mom, can you take these shots?" She claimed our various devices and snapped while we made Meriwether Lewis part of our gaiety.

While Dad sold a book to a passing stranger.

 The Old Trace meandered on our right, a dirt path bordered by a wooden fence and forest. Amidst our laughter, I imagined walking that path. Somber. Alone. I hugged my new friends and knew they saved me. They infused my Meriwether Lewis experience with joy.

But as we walked to the car, I looked back at Merry's marker and stood where he died.

Rock whispered secrets. It recorded the voices of Time. But nobody revealed the hidden elements of Meriwether Lewis's death. Merry accepted my nickel offering and gave me a greater gift.

I finally understood Lewis's connection to my father. They both feared a wasted life, always believing they could use what they were given to do more. When my father withdrew into himself, I read his thoughts. I understood them, because they mirrored mine. I walked almost 400 miles to find my father. The Natchez Trace was the portal.

When I read Meriwether Lewis's words, I saw my father and identified most everyone in my life. Because ambition makes anyone believe she never accomplishes enough. Dreamers always think they can do more to set passion free. My father morphed in that moment, because I could finally see him through a clear lens.

The lens of myself.

GO WALKING DOWN THERE
Chris Isaak

"I've stayed at this place before, Dad. It'll be fine." We navigated the dirt driveway of Creekview Farm near Fly, Tennessee.

"Never knew there was a place called Fly," Dad muttered as we hung a left at a y-junction.

"Just don't hit the peacocks, Mom."

"Peacocks?" Dad's quarter-sized bald spot danced as he gripped the dashboard. "I just hope the TV works."

I mopped my sweat-stained seat with a spare shirt. The gods of the Natchez Trace were legendary for extremes. They didn't spare me. My first days, I walked through pellets of sleet. Temperatures approached ninety degrees on my next-to-last fifteen mile day. Warmth helped with stiff joints and sore muscles. I stooped to take a picture at milepost 400 and almost levitated. When my parents found me at milepost 410, my only care was the joy that buzzed through my core. In spite of obstacles and crippling pain, I was almost to Nashville.

Creekview Farm, our last stop, was an outfitted house. After weeks of sharing bedrooms and cramming our stuff into small suites, we spread out in our own spaces, prepared dinner in a pristine kitchen and rocked on a screened porch. I walked across the threshold and found a home.

While I experienced rapture, Dad dawdled at the

foot of the stairs. He banged his fist against solid oak. "I can't believe I got more stairs. Can't I take this room down here?" He shuffled into the ground floor master bedroom.

"No. Kristen and Cooper have that room tonight, and somebody else reserved it tomorrow."

Cooper was my two-year-old guideson. His parents asked me to play the role of guidemother before he was born. A guidemother harbored no religious component. Instead, Kristen wanted me to teach her child to embrace experiences, to be curious, to make choices that would enrich his life.

He was born in the Hudson River Valley, and he sent his mother into labor on my wedding anniversary. Given the circuitous flight patterns between my home and his, I almost never saw him. Online, he transformed from newborn troll to cherub.

His parents asked me to make him curious about the world. I wanted them to know they chose the best person to fill their son with wonder.

Maybe Kristen believed I was capable of being Cooper's guidemother because I always cheered her dreams. We met when we were cast in the same play. Kristen was years younger, but we forged a friendship that survived her New York relocation. Even though I knew the long odds of winning theatrical parts, I told her not to give up, to go after what she wanted.

And, in the cast of a psychedelic Richard Foreman show, she met a man. And she married him. Her choice had nothing to do with me, but when she first told me about him, I exclaimed, "Forget everyone else. This is the man you should be with." He worshipped her, nourished her tender spirit and fought for her.

Because of our connection, Kristen wanted Cooper to walk a portion of the Natchez Trace with me. As soon as she messaged me with their schedule, I whiplashed between elation and panic. A curious toddler weaving alongside a federal highway? Without a guard rail or any protection from oncoming vehicles? I imagined tabloid stories and winced:

- *Guidemother Jailed In Child Endangerment Case. Should She Be Stoned?* -

While I waited for Kristen and Cooper, I relived my journey. Twelve different bedrooms in a month. Twelve sets of strangers befriended. Twelve kinds of hospitality. Even twelve brands of toilet paper.

Twelve times twelve times twelve times.......the math leaked into every part of me. I collapsed on the quilted bed, spent by the arithmetic of change. I couldn't imagine what I'd done to Dad. He flipped through TV channels, alternating static and random shows. "Thanks for sticking it out on this adventure, Dad," I whispered. "For helping me understand me. And you. And Meriwether Lewis."

Dad's voice careened up the stairs. "Andra! I done sold that Mr. Fly a book earlier today, and you got to go sign it."

"Dad—" I charged to the landing, my stained overshirt in one hand.

"Now, don't you go getting undressed. I'm taking you back down there right now, and you're gonna sign his book."

"But Dad, I'm exhausted, and—"

He held up a hand. "I don't wanna hear it. You're looking at exhausted." He tapped his own chest. "Right here. Now come on."

I marched downstairs like I was thirteen. Outside, I flung myself into the passenger seat. "I don't understand why we have to do this now."

"Because. I promised him we would. Now just be quiet, Andra. You got to buck up." He steered the car through the narrow gate. "You won't get to be a famous author by disappointing people. By being too lazy to sign their books. You got to make time for people, even when you don't feel like it. When you're famous, and you're gonna be famous, I don't want no one saying your old daddy didn't teach you how to treat people."

"I'm not going to be famous, Dad. And besides, people don't care about autographs anymore."

"It's not about that. You got to treat people like they matter. Like they're the only thing in your world. You do that, and you'll sell books, because people'll remember how you treat 'em. Just like they can't forget me."

"Dad, I—"

But he shifted to something else. "Have I told you

that story about when I was a Bible salesman and came on that farmer in south Georgia?"

I patted his arm. "Why don't you tell it again, Dad?"

PERSONAL JESUS
Depeche Mode

I was good at selling books, 'cause I didn't take no for an answer. Them Southwestern folks in Nashville taught us that. For three summers in college, I used their training to sell Bibles and other books door-to-door.

At my best, I never beat the lead guy. A stutterer, he was. He knocked on a door, and when the person said they wouldn't buy a Bible, he said, "M-m-m-m-m-mind if I r-r-r-r-r-r-r-ead it to y-y-y-y-y-you?"

Most people bought something to get rid of him. I learned a lot from his technique.

Take the time I was in South Georgia.

It was a hundred and ten degrees in the shade, and I was driving around the countryside, trying to find a customer. I pulled up next to this farmer with a bunch of mules, and I got out and walked into his dusty field.

He wasn't happy to see me. Before I could even ask him to buy the Good Book, he let loose with a stream of profanity. Cussed me up one side and down the other, and told me where I could stick my Bible.

I tried to get a word in edgewise, but he wasn't having none of it. Kept cussing me 'til I was in my car.

Well, let me tell you, I was down on my quota for the week, and I didn't know what I was gonna do. I saw one final house set off the road, and I pulled up in there, thinking I might find somebody home.

A gray-headed woman answered the door, surrounded by I-don't-know-how-many kids. Husband wasn't there, she said, but she listened while I gave her my sales speech and showed her my best family Bible. When I was done, she smiled. "Wait right here."

She came back with fifty dollars, my sales requirement for the whole week. "I'll take whatever this'll buy."

People say it takes a miracle to sell books. That may be true. But I know my daughter's got miracles on her side, 'cause I done seen a few.

LOVE WALKS IN
Van Halen

"Don't pinch him, Dad. Why do you always pinch?"

Cooper squirmed away from Dad and ran toward the bedroom, his distended diaper smacking chubby legs.

"Why don't we get that nasty diaper off you, Coop." Everything squished when he plopped on the hardwood floor, and I exercised a guide-mother's prerogative. "Okay. Your mother can do it."

I left him picking his diaper's foul edges and found Mom in the kitchen, scrubbing the counter. Dad slept in front of the television. Volume vibrated my eyeballs.

Cooper steamrolled between us in a fresh outfit spangled with trains. High octane rocket fuel and layers of skin. I ran my fingers through fine-spun blonde hair as he funnel-clouded toward Dad. Energy magnified the chasm between Life's beginning and end. I hugged Mom. "I don't want to lose you and Dad. I mean, I know that's silly, because it's inevitable, and I get that, but—"

"You've had your father almost thirty years longer than I had mine."

I didn't want to finish, because my dwindling walk represented the milestones of Life.

I stared into the morning of my last fifteen mile day. No more stiff, too-early wake-up calls. Five hours of peace and pain. The final night of my adventure with my

father. We'd share our last country breakfast the next morning, before we loaded the car.

I wished Time worked like a mental camera, with a button to freeze the frames.

Cooper tugged my fingers, and I hoisted him to my hip. "Go see the elephants?"

Peacocks preened along the driveway.

"Those aren't........no, wait." I kissed his ear. "We can go see as many elephants as you want. Dad!" I shouted into the living room. "Get ready. I need to be on the road by ten."

His belly sliced the front of his pajamas, and he gripped the leather sofa with both hands. Maybe he wanted to stop Time, too.

When he shuffled up the stairs, I ached with every labored step. "Dad. Do you need help?"

"Nah. I—" He slid his foot to another step and huffed. "I got it."

When Mom dropped Kristen and Cooper to walk with me, Dad occupied his usual seat. The car listed to the right as they drove up the highway. "I just love your parents, Andra." Kristen waited while I slipped Cooper into a cloth backpack. "Coop does, too. Your mom was telling him that story."

"Which one?"

"About the teeny, tiny woman."

"Oh, yeah. I remember that one from when I was a kid."

"Coop laughed and laughed at her high-pitched voice."

"I always did, too."

She pushed chocolate-hued hair behind an ear. "Maybe they can be another set of grandparents to Cooper."

I left him and his mother at the War of 1812 memorial. Another ten miles on my own.

I waved to every passing vehicle. Spring lit up the Trace like blinking holiday lights. Green obliterated brown. Bees floated around my head, drunk on nectar.

As I approached a bridge, I took out my phone to

snap a record of a lone bicycle towing a cart. Cyclists rode the length of the Trace in a week. An extended winter kept me bereft of their company for much of my walk.

I stopped next to the abandoned bike. From my own Trace experience, I knew better than to explore under an overpass. The bike's owner might be down there, using Nature as a toilet. For the same reason, I avoided a perusal of the trees ringing the highway. Everybody deserved a private place to relieve themselves.

Before I took another step, a man streaked from the woods, his arms raised over his head. "I'm the ghost of Meriwether Lewis," he belted in deep monotone, while I stood frozen. Closer and closer, the ghost-man came. When he was two feet from me, he whipped one hand behind his back and produced a copy of my novel. "The ghost of Meriwether Lewis would like you to sign his book."

I took in his fuzzy white beard. His sunburn. His cyclist lycra. "Is this your bicycle?"

He unsnapped his helmet and scratched his head. "Dang it. I promised your dad I'd hide in the woods and pretend I was the ghost of Meriwether Lewis. Don't tell him I didn't scare you."

"Oh, you scared me. You don't know how many brushes I've had with his ghost." I took a drag from my CamelBak. "I'm Andra."

"Tom. I'm riding the Trace for my seventy-fifth birthday."

"All the way to Natchez?"

He handed me a pen and waited while I scrawled my name on a page. "Yeah. Figured an epic bike trip might be just the thing to ring in a milestone birthday, 'cause when you get to be my age, you never know which one of these'll be the last."

"Well, when you get to Natchez, you have to stay with Miss Ethel."

"Oh, your dad already told me about her. Sounds like the perfect way to end this crazy adventure."

"Or to begin one. She's up for anything."

He zipped my novel into his pack and shook my hand. "I'm looking forward to reading your book while

I camp."

I gripped his palm an extra second. "Whatever you do, I hope this year brings Life's grandest moments."

"Thanks. Hope I didn't spook you."

Before I could reassure him, he tipped his helmet and disappeared, while I scanned the skyline and listened for his pedal squeaks.

Birdsong trilled through trees.

I stared at nothing and wondered how many ghosts I met on the Natchez Trace.

My last fifteen mile day came too soon. And, just like when I started, my phone lit up with messages from readers all over the world.

> I knew you had this.

> You're a badass.

> Almost there! Tomorrow's the day!

> Make sure to savor it.

Mileposts ticked past, and I zipped my phone camera into my pocket and recorded the world with my senses instead. Cut grass and manure. Slight changes in slope. Migrating birds and tufts of pink on red bud trees. Life would no longer be hearing without listening, scents without smell. I licked my lips to taste salt film, and I ran my hands along white numbered mileposts.

I was full. I overflowed with the joy of Life.

But as I climbed into the car and stretched my legs, I didn't mourn the end of daily fifteen mile meditations. The road blitzed by the window, a watercolor painting. Incomplete. Wherever our lives ended, I could still make

memories with my father. Plan time with my parents. Add another pushpin to anticipate in Life's timeline. We didn't have to take five-week car trips. Experiences added up in hour-long walks. Weekend excursions. Memories we built into the busy monotony of Life.

Hours later, I prepared for my last Trace night. Dad

fingered the chrome grille of a Model A and exclaimed, "That's some car."

It belonged to a couple celebrating their fiftieth anniversary by driving the Trace. I took pictures while Dad sold them a book.

Before they went inside, the woman slipped a wisp of green into my hand.

"A four leaf clover," I breathed and caressed downy petals. "I can't take this."

"I find them all the time." She smiled. "How do you think I've stayed married fifty years?"

I thanked her as she and her husband closed their bedroom door, the room Kristen and Cooper occupied the night before. While Dad settled at the television, I dragged myself upstairs for one final soak in the tub.

I hummed with bliss. With accomplishment. Yet, I was a failure, though I didn't know it. I wanted to finish my walk with the headline

- Debut Novelist Walks Her Way to Best Seller -

I would complete my last day with five hundred books sold. Slightly more than one book per mile.

And I didn't care. My mental sky was lit with five weeks of memories, time with my parents nobody could erase. Gifted minutes. Millions of seconds to match my million steps. My hours built days that bloomed into five weeks, seasoned with lessons in joy. I was determined not to stand over my parents' caskets and whisper, "I wish we'd done............"

Life is about what happens between all the things we wish we'd done. And when we do those things, Life fills holes and lights the flame of wishes. Life makes wishes live.

Not Without My Father

LEARNING TO FLY

Tom Petty

"Last bit's gonna be hilly, Andra." Dad yelled from his window while Mom snapped a photo of me walking away from milepost 435. My last day walking the Natchez Trace.

"Nine miles to go. I'll see you at the end."

Mom slipped my iPhone into my hand. "We'll stay with you today, Andra. You know, in case you need us."

I swallowed the burn in my throat and turned before she could see my face. "Okay."

Air bulged with the promise of rain. I wove along the highway, one eye on the purple bruise spreading across the sky. My phone jangled through a thunderclap.

"Andra Watkins."

"Can I speak to Andre Watson?"

Sigh. "Speaking."

A male voice continued. "This is News Channel 4 in Nashville. We're coming out to interview you, but we can't get there until 1. Can you make the walk last that long in this weather?"

I pulled the phone from my ear and checked the time. Eleven o'clock in the morning. Two hours to walk nine miles.

I laughed. "Yep. I can't wait to meet you."

"We'll just find you if the weather holds. Don't worry about being somewhere specific. If you see us, you see us."

I ended the call and squealed. I was going be on Nashville TV.

Maybe?

Adrenaline flooded my insides, a nerve-and-nausea cocktail I battled whenever I stood in the wings, awaiting my entrance in a play.

Before I took a step, the phone mewed again.

"Andra Watkins."

A female voice chirped in my ear. "Hi, this is Alex from *The Tennessean.* I want to be there when you wrap up today. When'll that be?"

"Two," I blurted before I did mental calculations. Frantic, I added up time and hoped everything came out right.

Call waiting beeped through our goodbye.

"Hello?"

"Andra. It's Michael." My husband was on his way into Nashville to pick up supplies for an event at Parnassus Books. My first official appearance as a published author.

"Hey, Dear. So much is happening. I've got a TV station coming out and—"

"Well, you might want to shake up your schedule."

"Why?"

"Because, when I drove through the gate at the end of the Trace, the last milepost was 442."

"What? How can that be?" I dragged out my rumpled Trace map and read the words, 'The northern terminus, milepost 444, is near Nashville, TN.' Was the Parkway map a lie? "Everything says it's 444 miles."

"I know. I scoured my map, too, and I drove it, just to make sure. Even stopped and asked somebody."

"And?"

"Four forty-two is the end."

Rain blotched my face. The atmosphere was a giant water balloon, and Trace spirits hovered, ready to throw it my way. "So, I've got to make six more miles last three hours?"

"Just finish whenever, Andra. Timing doesn't matter."

"It does, though. There's the TV at one. Newspaper at two." My voice trilled upward, a crescendo of panic. After five weeks without a set schedule, two appointments threatened to undo me. A raindrop landed on my nose, and I watched it, cross-eyed. It skittered down the front of my green jacket and disappeared.

A little girl with blonde curls knocked inside my head. I spent more than a year with her, writing her story. She started in a courtroom with a bead of sweat running down her nose. I would end my tale with a snout full of rain. I wiped my face and laughed.

"What's funny?"

"Oh, nothing. I wanted this day to last. I guess now I've got an excuse to take my time."

"What about the weather?"

"Dear, I can walk through anything."

An hour later, I walked up to the bridge near milepost 438. I stood on the edge and looked down. Grass and highway spun together, a gaping infinity. I wasn't sure I could cross it. The guardrail didn't reach my waist as I took a few tentative steps onto its southern end. Sky and trees and asphalt collided with vertigo. I wound up on my stomach. A cold expansion joint zippered across pavement. My knuckles scraped against cardboard, and when I closed my hands around a box, I focused on its lettering—*Fix A Flat*—to lift me to unsteady feet.

"You saved a bike. Maybe you saved my life." I threw the box on the ground and took a picture. Before I looked down again, I snapped several more. The gentle angle of the roadbed. Toothy metal. A lone figure on the other side.

My mother. I kept my eyes on her, a worthy competitor to the glory of Birdsong Hollow. Because, sometimes, being in the moment meant not looking down.

I wobbled away from the northern end of the bridge and caught Dad in exquisite form. His last sale on the

Trace. A motorcyclist. A pull-off. A person and a parking lot were all he needed to pounce.

He wagged my book in the man's face. "She wrote this book here. See?"

I walked over and offered my hand. "Hi. I'm Andra. Are you riding the whole Trace alone?"

"Aw. I couldn't compete with your walking it. Your dad here's been filling me in. But no. I'm just out for a joy ride."

"Tell me about your bike."

I listened to his stories about riding. About Vietnam. About living.

"I'll take one of your books." He unzipped a black satchel and made room.

Maybe I could sell books, too.

As I high-fived Dad, I realized we were a team. He moved in for the pitch, and I closed the sale. How would my writing career ever survive without my father?

I pottered into the road, my home for more than a month, my thoughts consumed with images of Dad. His triple-chinned laughter. The cadence of his voice. His habit of turning off his hearing aids.

I waved to the TV van and breezed through my interview. When they told me to walk along the highway while they filmed me, my body did what it needed to do. I left them to navigate my final downhill, my twisting approach into Nashville, but I wanted to dig my heels into pavement and stop Time. I vowed to live pain and wonder again if my parents did it with me. I started my trek dreading every second with them. When did our relationship agony morph into ecstasy?

"Ma'am. You okay?" A man sat in a white SUV, his mouth obscured by a handlebar mustache. I took in the logo on the side of his ride. A federal ranger. The first one I'd encountered since Jackson, Mississippi, three-fourths of the Natchez Trace Parkway.

"I'm great. Been walking the Trace. This is my last day."

"You come all the way from Natchez?" He leaned through the window and ran his fingers over the United

States Government emblem.

"Yeah. I started March 1." I held my breath and waited. Rangers south of Jackson greeted me with doubt. One even regaled me with the story of a couple who tried a through hike, only to be washed out at milepost 90. His tone dripped with, "And they were more fit than you."

The first federal employee to admit I might succeed was a surveyor at milepost 222. It was radio silence from there.

He pounded his door. "We been talking about you for weeks! The maintenance crews have been cut back and all that—budget nonsense, you understand—but they've been doing extra runs without pay just for you. 'Gotta check on our girl!' Every day, they've been following your trek on their own time."

"Really?" I thought about the trash collectors I came upon at pull-offs, the foresters I encountered as they removed fallen trees and debris. The trucks that honked as they rattled past. When I talked to them, they said they were doing their jobs as well as they could with no funding, trying to preserve a forgotten place. I blinked back tears with the realization that underpaid, unappreciated people gave their own time and resources to make sure I was safe. To pave the way for me to finish. I swallowed. "Everybody's been following me?"

"Yep. I'm so glad I got to meet you. And you're finishing today."

Still shell-shocked, I nodded. "In about a mile. Yes."

"Well. Good luck to you. We're all rooting for you, wherever you go from here."

His taillights faded into rain, and I whispered, "Wherever I go from here."

I walked over a short bridge. Along a wooden fence. To milepost 442. The official end of the Natchez Trace Parkway.

But I found a new beginning.

I WOULD WALK 500 MILES
The Proclaimers

What did I expect to feel as I walked through a wooden gate and hoisted my foot onto milepost 442, the end of the Natchez Trace? I knew I'd see Michael and my parents. Even the reporter from *The Tennessean*.

But I didn't realize my friend Cindy Duryea would drive twelve hours from South Carolina, didn't know she stopped in Aiken to pick up her eighty-nine-year-old mother. I never knew she called her Nashville-based daughter Katy from the car to say, "I just picked Mom up. Now, we're on our way to get you and meet Andra, and won't that be something?"

I experienced my walk's greatest gift at the finish line. Hugging Cindy and knowing my journey inspired someone else's adventure. She knew she didn't need five weeks. She took twenty-four hours and did something spontaneous with people she loved.

I smiled for the camera and wondered what would happen if more people copied Cindy? For a few hours. A couple of days. Maybe even a week. Memories could be stamped on any unexpected outing with people who mattered.

It's only too late to make memories when it's too late.

As everyone gathered around me, I couldn't feel anything. For the first time in five weeks, nothing hurt. My body was numb.

But my mind buzzed with the trip's revelations about

Mom. About Dad. About myself. My heart overflowed with joy. I nodded to ghosts who detoured from the traditional Trace route and stood by my side.

Because the last seven miles of the Natchez Trace Parkway were a new road. Around Nashville the Old Trace was consumed by development years ago. When I nodded to the boatmen, I knew they came because they wanted to be there.

After almost an hour of celebrating, people peeled away, and I was left with Michael, Mom and Dad.

"I'd like to go to that big stone sign a couple of miles back and take some pictures."

I wasn't ready to say goodbye to the Natchez Trace.

We piled into two vehicles and drove through misting rain. When I looked into the trees, I was transported to points on the Trace's 10,000 year timeline. I focused on hardwood and leaves and slivers of sky, and for a few seconds, if I closed my eyes, I traveled through Time.

For 442 miles, I tried to honor the countless men who walked the Natchez Trace, alone or in packs, to build the frontier states of the USA. I listened to the voices of Native Americans who were displaced. "See what we did?" They whispered from ancient mounds and buried places. Quebecois French mingled with conquistador Spanish on the wings of thousands of migrating birds. I heard sounds I didn't recognize, rhythms I never expected. And, at the end, I only had one plea.

I hoped the Trace seared us into its soul. When people traveled it in a thousand years, maybe a few of them would hear my parents and me. In fallen leaves and birdsong. In the echo of their own footsteps. In a field of daffodils winking in the breeze.

I stood next to the Natchez Trace Parkway sign, flanked by my parents.

 When I smiled into the camera, with one arm around each of them, I made one final addendum.

I wanted to recall every molecule of our adventure. The sound of my father's laugh. How my mother said my name. Through tears, I hugged my parents and branded them into the corridors of my brain.

Because when someone remembers us, we live forever.

Not Without My Father

EPILOGUE
MAKE A MEMORY
Bon Jovi

Who matters to you? Maybe you're like me, with aging parents who are still somewhat healthy. Or perhaps this story finds you near Life's end, with adult children and grandchildren.

We can all name people we take for granted, because everybody's swamped. Overwhelmed. Harried. We mean to make memories with people who matter, but often, we put it off for someday. And someday morphs into never, as Life's unpredictability claims the people we love.

I wrote *Not Without My Father* to inspire others to make a memory. Now. Today. To grab someone and turn "I wish I had" into "I'm glad I did."

If you enjoyed this story, the best tribute you can pay lies in making a memory of your own. You don't have to spend five weeks. Take an hour. Or an afternoon. A day or several.

Make a Memory is a MOVEMENT.

Help start it by making your own memory.

- Post a picture or video online.
- Include your name, where you live, and who you're inviting to make a memory.
- Show the memory you want to make with a photo, a map, a gif or a video. Be creative. Make everyone who sees it want to Make this Memory

with you.

- Tag the person you're inviting to Make a Memory so they can respond.
- Hashtag your post with #NWMFMakeaMemory.

We'll collect your Make a Memory submissions and showcase them on andrawatkins.com.

This isn't a contest to impress everyone with your grand travel aspirations or lofty goals. It's a sincere plea to spend time with someone who matters, to be able to say "I'm glad I did." If you need ideas, go to andrawatkins.com/makeamemory.

Your Make a Memory entry could change your life.

But your participation will help make enough memories to change the world.

ACKNOWLEDGEMENTS

Books come to life because of the people who care about them. *Not Without My Father* is a tour de force of caring. I have a village of people to thank.

Michael T Maher, you are the most supportive husband on the planet. You believe in me when belief fails me. I couldn't do anything without you.

Alice Guess, you signed up for this craziness early, and you never wavered. You got me through my first week of walking, and you messaged me every day when you left. I never would've made it to the end without you. Thanks to Gordon and Cayleigh for sharing you with me.

Lisa Kramer and Tori Nelson, you made two days on the Trace hilarious. Tori, thanks to you, Tom and Thomas for putting us up for four days at the end of my walk.

Kristen and Cooper Cronin, I love you both. Thank you for making memories with me.

Jessie Powell and Scott Merriman, thank you for making the trek to Tennessee to meet me.

Cindy Duryea and Katy Duryea, thank you for surprising me at the Nashville finish line with Kitty Windham (Cindy's mom and Katy's grandmother). We lost Kitty on November 1, 2014. She died peacefully, driving and doing and going until her last day. I'm even more grateful Cindy chose to make this memory.

Mary Howard and Stephen King of Tupelo, Mississippi, thank you for taking in a complete stranger for dinner. I loved spending an evening with you. And thanks to

Stephen's sister Angie King Keesee for making the connection.

Numerous women texted and emailed words of encouragement during my trek. Thanks to Mary Giese, Linda Washington, Nancy Teixeira, Lisa Kennedy, and especially Laurence King, whose messages often found me at my worst moments.

Randy Fought at Natchez Trace Travel, thank you for your patience with numerous questions and last-minute changes. I never could've planned accommodations on my own. You took care of everything. Whenever I need a place to stay on the Natchez Trace, I won't look anywhere else.

Trace innkeepers were my salvation. You washed clothes, accommodated Dad's food requests, ran errands and saw to our every need. Here's to a stellar group of people: Ethel Banta at Hope Farm in Natchez, Mississippi; Bobbye and Phil Pinnix at Isabella Bed and Breakfast in Port Gibson, Mississippi; Brenda and Charles Davis at Mamie's Cottage in Raymond, Mississippi; Larry Routt at Maple Terrace Inn in Kosciusko, Mississippi; Summer Poche at French Camp Bed and Breakfast in French Camp, Mississippi; Carol Koutroulis at Bridges Hall Manor in Houston, Mississippi; Pat and Ron Deaton at Belmont Hotel in Belmont, Mississippi; Linda and David Rochelle at Coast to Coast Store in Collinwood, Tennessee; Donna Branch at Buffalo River Farm Bed and Breakfast in Summertown, Tennessee; and Misty Montgomery at Creekview Farm Bed and Breakfast in Fly, Tennessee. If any reader would like to replicate our journey, our rooms are listed in the appendix.

Culinary surprises were among the biggest delights of my walk. Because I couldn't mention them all in the book, I share them here. I ended my first day at The Malt Shop in Natchez, Mississippi with the best chocolate malt I've ever had. Mister D at Old Country Store in Lorman, Mississippi, you really do make heavenly fried chicken, and you sing like a  dream. Mary Bell and the crew at Gibbes Old Country Store in Learned, Mississippi, I still drool when I think of your steaks, and your Comeback sauce was the best of the trip. After Dad grumbled about eating at the Mayflower Cafe in Jackson, Mississippi, I couldn't drag him out. The folks at the Council House Cafe in French Camp, Mississippi fed me several sandwiches, and their Mississippi Mud Pie was heaven. Costa Oaxaquena in Belmont, Mississippi, your shrimp quesadillas were addictive pillows of goodness. Red Bay, Alabama's Cardinal Drive-in supplied my birthday milkshake. For three days, we ate every meal at Chad's Family Restaurant in Collinwood, Tennessee. I was willing to make the drive to Mt Pleasant Grille in Mt Pleasant, Tennessee again and again. Finally, thanks to Nashville's City House for introducing us to Paul, our server with Lewis and Clark tattoos, a gift that made our celebration meal surreal.

Thanks to everyone who gave me song ideas, especially Dina Honour (Walkin' After Midnight), Beth Kennedy (Learning to Fly), Kate Pitt (Holiday Road), Lou Mello (Walk On By), Lisa Kramer (I'm Gonna Be and A Million Miles Away), Rob Ross (Personal Jesus), Andrea Boccucci (Walk), Robert S Johnson (Cross Road Blues and Road to Nowhere), Kirsten Piccini (Love Walks In), Linda Washington (I Walk the Line), Penny O'Neill (Hit the Road Jack), Kenneth Andrews (Go Walking Down There), Alice Guess (Walking to You), Nancy Teixeira (These Boots Were Made for Walkin'), Debbie Hennessy (Walking on Broken Glass), Cheryl Smithem (Roam), Debra Fetterly (Walk on the Wild Side), Helena Hann-Basquiat (Walk Like an Egyptian) and Lisa Spiral Besnett (Walking on Sunshine).

To the women and men who work for the National Park Service and the National Forest Service, you are unsung heroes. Thank you for everything you do to protect our assets, often with very limited means. Your sacrifices are not celebrated enough.

Thanks to the people at the *Kosciusko Star-Herald*, Nashville's News Channel 4, *The Tennessean* and *The Post and Courier* for covering parts of my walk.

Amber Deutsch, you continue to make my books better by reading them first. Your tireless commentary and quirky insights are priceless, as is your friendship.

Rowe Copeland, your edits made *Not Without My Father* readable. Thank you.

Two authors deserve thanks for inspiring my walk of

the Natchez Trace. Keel Hunt's book *Coup: The Day the Democrats Ousted Their Governor, Put Republican Lamar Alexander in Office Early, and Stopped a Pardon Scandal* gave me the idea to walk the Trace. James Crutchfield's *Natchez Trace: A Pictorial History* was a valuable planning tool.

Tamie and Sam Herin, thank you for loaning me your house in Montreat, North Carolina. Every version of this book was written on Mississippi Road, an irony that isn't lost on me. Be Still is a place of perfect peace.

Ed Smith, thank you for giving us a place to sleep on yet another Trace visit.

Ruth Sykora and Stephen Khouri, you massaged and adjusted my middle-aged body into a machine. Thank you for your touch.

Joyce Maher, you know what you did. Thank you for being the world's best mother-in-law.

Thanks to the team at Nashville's Parnassus Books for hosting a nobody-writer's first book signing and end-of-walk party. You are a gem of an independent bookstore.

Jeffrey Nelson, thank you for having your daughter Tori. I wish I could've met you.

My mother, Linda Watkins, gave me three weeks of her life and probably felt like she was minding a four-year-old again. Thanks, Mom, for everything you did to feed, clothe, bathe, and generally comfort your crazy daughter. I love you.

Without my father, Roy Lee Watkins Junior, this book wouldn't be possible. Dad, you pushed yourself through whatever the Trace gave you, and you spread your unique brand of joy over three states. Thank you for saying yes to an adventure with me. Thank you for everything you did to make it memorable. Thank you for being the best book salesman of all time. But mostly, thank you for being my father. You are a gift to me. Every

day. I love you.

To readers everywhere, thank you for choosing this book. If you've read this far, you're a diehard. We writers cannot create without people like you. In a world bursting with options, thank you for honoring me with your time.

SUPPORT THE TRACE

Want to know the best way to support the Natchez Trace Parkway? Visit!

Plan a Trace vacation and explore a tunnel through Time. More visitors mean more voices. You can force our legislators to provide more money to maintain the Parkway.

Randy Fought at Natchez Trace Travel can plan a trip to suit any interest. Contact him at natcheztracetravel.com/

Want to sleep where we did? Here's a cheat sheet of the rooms we occupied along the Trace.

- Hope Farm in Natchez, MS - Plantation Room
- Isabella Bed and Breakfast in Port Gibson, MS - Lucille's Room in the main house (the room I wanted, not the one Dad picked elsewhere)
- Mamie's Cottage Bed and Breakfast at the Dupree House in Raymond, MS - Pattie Dupree Suite
- Maple Terrace Inn in Kosciusko, MS - Silkwood and Mahogany Rooms
- French Camp Bed and Breakfast in French Camp, MS - B&B Junior Cabin
- Bridges Hall Manor in Houston, MS - Room 4
- Belmont Hotel in Belmont, MS - Rooms 7 and 9
- Coast to Coast Store in Collinwood, TN - Room 2
- Buffalo River Farm and Studio Bed and Breakfast in Summertown, TN - Robert E Lee and Abraham

Lincoln Rooms
- Creekview Farm Retreat Bed and Breakfast in Fly, TN - both upstairs bedrooms

Because of continued cuts in government funding, the Natchez Trace Parkway increasingly relies upon donations to fund its dwindling budget. You can help preserve a 10,000-year-old treasure. Your contributions could provide much-needed restroom facilities, refurbished parking areas, increased staffing for road maintenance and trash removal, more ranger patrols, and replacement signage, not to mention better facilities for the thousands of people who bicycle the Trace each year.

Help the Trace retain its magic. To support the Natchez Trace Parkway, go to: http://www.nps.gov/natr/supportyourpark/donate.htm

I have.

ABOUT THE AUTHOR

Andra Watkins lives in Charleston, South Carolina with her husband, Michael T Maher. A non-practicing CPA, she has a degree in accounting from Francis Marion University. She's still mad at her mother for refusing to let her major in musical theater, because her mom was convinced she'd end up starring in porn films. Her acclaimed first novel *To Live Forever: An Afterlife Journey of Meriwether Lewis* was published by Word Hermit Press on March 1, 2014. Read more about Andra at andrawatkins.com.

Andra's upcoming novels include *Building Castles in the Air: An Afterlife Journey of Theodosia Burr Alston*, to be published in Spring 2016.

Natchez Trace: Tracks in Time is a book of photographs taken by Andra on her 444-mile walk. It is a companion volume to *Not Without My Father*, and is available in print from Amazon, Barnes & Noble, and everywhere books are sold.

TO LIVE FOREVER:
AN AFTERLIFE JOURNEY OF MERIWETHER LEWIS
(The novel that launched a 444-Mile Hike)

EMMALINE

A New Orleans Courtroom
Thursday
March 24, 1977

A drop of sweat hung from the end of my nose. I watched it build, cross-eyed, before I shook my head and made it fall. It left wet circles on the front of my dress.

"Emmaline. Be still, Child." Aunt Bertie fanned her face and neck with a paper fan, the one with the popsicle stick handle.

A popsicle would be so good.

The waiting room of the court in New Orleans was full. People were everywhere I looked.

Reporters in stripey suits talked with some of Daddy's musician friends. I loved to watch their fingers play imaginary guitars or pound out chords on their legs. Once or twice, Daddy's band members came over to squeeze my arm or pat my head. "In spite of what they's saying in that courtroom, we all love your daddy, Kid."

Everybody loved Daddy. Well, everybody except Mommy.

My nose burned when I breathed, because the whole room stank like sweaty feet. My face was steamy when I touched it, and my lace tights scratched when I kicked my legs to push along the wooden bench. I left a puddle when I moved.

I snuggled closer to the dark folds and softness of Aunt Bertie. She turned her black eyes down at me and sighed before pushing me away with her dimpled hand. "Too hot, Child. When this is done, I'll hold you as long as you want."

I slid back to my wet spot on the bench. The wood made a hard pillow when I leaned my head against it and closed my eyes. Wishes still worked for nine-year-old girls, didn't they?

I thought and thought. If I wanted it enough, maybe I could shrink myself smaller. It was hard to be outside the courtroom, imagining what was going on inside. Behind the heavy doors, Mommy and Daddy probably shouted mean things at each other, like they used to at home. Both of them said they wanted me, if they had to fight until they were dead.

I watched Mommy's lady friends go into the courtroom: Miss Roberta in her drapey dress with flowers, Miss Chantelle all in white against the black of her skin, and Miss Emilie in a red skirt and coat that tied at her waist in a pretty bow. They all went in and came out, and they always looked at me. Miss Roberta even left a red lipstick kiss on my cheek, but I don't like her, so I rubbed it off.

Aunt Bertie took her turn inside the courtroom, leaving me to sit with a reporter. He watched me from behind thick black glasses, and he asked me all kinds of questions about Daddy and Mommy. I didn't understand much. I knew Daddy was famous, at least in New Orleans, but I didn't understand what the word "allegations" meant.

My daddy was Lee Cagney. People called him "The Virtuoso of Dixieland Jazz." He played the upright bass, and when he sang, his voice made women act silly in the middle of Bourbon Street. They cried and screamed. Some of them even tore their clothes.

I understood why women loved Daddy. I adored him, too. But some grown women sure did act dumb.

Anyway.

None of the lawyers asked me who I wanted to be with.

The Judge said I was too little to understand, and Mommy agreed. But if they asked me, I would shout it all the way to Heaven: I wanted to be with Daddy.

When he sang *Ragtime Lullaby*, the sound of his voice put me to sleep. He always splashed in the fountain with me in front of the Cathedral and gave me pennies to throw in the water. Thursday afternoons before his gigs, he sat with me at Café du Monde, sharing beignets with as much powdered sugar as I wanted. He didn't even mind my sticky fingers when he held my hand. He wasn't always there when I had nightmares, but he came to see me first thing in the morning.

People around me whispered about Daddy's "adulterous proclivities." I didn't understand what that meant, but it had something to do with his loving other women besides Mommy. No matter what they said, Daddy didn't do anything wrong. When he wasn't playing music, he was always with me.

Wasn't he?

A skinny reporter held the courtroom door open. "The Judge's ruling." He whispered, but his voice was loud enough for everyone waiting to hear. He kept the door open, and I saw my chance.

I struggled through all the legs to the door. Mommy's red lips curled in a smile as the Judge addressed Daddy. The Judge's face was loose, like the bulldog that lived in the house around the corner, and his voice boomed in my chest. When he stood and leaned over his desk, his hairy hands gripped the gavel.

"In the case of Cagney v. Cagney, I am charged with finding the best outcome for a little girl. For rendering a verdict that will shape the whole of her life. The welfare of the child is paramount, regardless of how it will impact the adults involved."

The Judge stopped and cleared his throat. I held my breath when his baggy eyes fell on me. I counted ten heartbeats before he talked again. "Mr. Cagney, I simply cannot ignore the fact that you had carnal relations with your then-wife's lady friends repeatedly, both under your shared roof and in broad daylight. The photographic evidence coupled with the testimonies of these poor women damns you, regardless of your expressed love for your daughter. From everything I've seen and heard in this courtroom, the evidence does not support your claim that you were set up. Justice demands that your nine-year-old daughter be delivered into the arms of the person who has demonstrated that she has the capability to be a responsible parent."

He looked around the room and sat up straight in his chair. "I am granting sole custody of Emmaline Cagney to her mother, Nadine Cagney, and I hereby approve her request to block Lee Cagney from any and all contact with his daughter until she reaches the age of eighteen. Mr. Cagney, should you violate this directive, you will be found in contempt of this court, an offense that may be punishable by imprisonment of up to 120 days and a fine of no more than $500 per occurrence. This court is adjourned."

He pounded a wooden stick on his desk, and everyone swarmed like bees. Daddy stood up and shook his fist. He shouted at the Judge over all the other noise. "Lies! Set out to ruin my reputation—my memory—in the eyes of my daughter! I'll appeal, if I have to spend every dime of my money. I'll—"

The Judge banged his stick again, lots of times, while my eyes met Daddy's. I ran from the doorway. The room was like the obstacle course on the playground, only with people who reached for me while the Judge boomed, "Order! Order! I will have order in my court!"

Daddy's lawyer held him and whispered something in his ear. It was my chance. I ran toward Daddy and his crying blue eyes. They matched mine, because I was crying, too.

Daddy elbowed his lawyer into the railing and reached out his hand. "Come to me, Baby."

I kicked at pants legs and stomped on shiny shoes. At the front, I stuck my hand through the bars and stretched as far as I could. My fingers almost reached his when my head jerked like I was snagged at the end of a fishing pole.

Mommy had the ties at the back of my white pinafore. Her glossy red lips fake-smiled. "I'm taking Emmaline now, Lee. Good luck to you."

She squeezed my hand. Her red fingernails dug into my skin.

"Ow, Mommy. You're hurting me."

Her high heels clack-clack-clacked as she dragged me through the chairs and down the aisle toward the waiting room. I planted my heels and tried to get one last look, my mind taking a picture of Daddy. Before we got through the door, I saw his shoulders shake. Three policemen held him back and kept him from following me. The world was blurry like the time I swam to the bottom of a pool and opened my eyes underwater.

Mommy picked me up and cradled me in her arms. Her blood-tipped fingers stroked my hair, but her lips whispered a different story, one the crowd couldn't hear. "Stop crying, Emmaline. You know this is for the best." She shifted me to the ground and adjusted the wide sash of her floor-length dress. Its sleeves fanned out as she pushed the bar on the door. I wished she'd take off and fly away.

Summer heat turned my tears to steam, and my eyes ached. Mommy struggled to pull me along through the reporters that blocked the path to the car. They shouted questions, but I didn't hear them. All I heard were Daddy's words. "Come to me, Baby."

Mommy smiled and pressed our bodies through the people. She kept her gaze glued on the car.

Aunt Bertie waited behind the wheel of Mommy's fancy red Cadillac Eldorado. Mommy always said the whole name with a funny accent. The engine was running. "There's Bertie. In you go, Emmaline. I'm ready to be done with this madness."

My legs squeaked across the hot back seat. Mommy ran her fingers under my eyes to wipe away my tears, but they kept coming. "Please. You're upsetting my daughter." She shouted over her shoulder.

The door slammed, and it was like a clock stopped. Like I would never be older than that moment. Everything would always be "Before Daddy" and "After Daddy."

Daddy.

His face appeared in the slice of back window. I put down the glass, trying to slip through, but Mommy ran around the car. She screamed and hit him, over and over. "You stay away from her, Lee! You heard what the Judge said!"

Her black hair fell out of its bun as she pounded him with her fists. He tried to move away from her. Toward me. He reached his hand through the window and touched my face. His mouth opened to speak to me, but a policeman came up behind him and dragged him away from the car.

"I'll write you, Emmaline! Every day. I promise," he shouted. "I'll prove these things aren't true! I'll give up everything to be with you!" The policeman pushed him through the courthouse door, and he was gone.

"I'll write you, too, Daddy." I whispered it, soft so nobody but God or my guardian angel could hear. "Somehow, I'll make us be together again."

THE JUDGE

I leaned my weight against an upstairs window, the ruckus of her daddy's court still unfolding on the other side of a bolted door. Breath ragged. White film on glass. Wet tracks trailed from my fingers, the record of my need.

My craving.

Had I waited too long to see her again? I used to watch her. How she played hopscotch on a broken slab of sidewalk. Colored chalk and creamy skin and sing-song. I stood in the shadows until I was sure. Until I knew it was her.

My little beauty. It was my name for her. Before. In another life.

She never saw me. All those times, I hid. I waited. I scribbled letters in cipher, that code we always used, but I never mailed them. Patience would yield to my desire. For as long as I could remember, all I had to do was wait for weakness to reveal the path.

That was before I saw her today.

Eye contact was electricity. It surged through my limbs and soared around my heart. She looked at me, and she knew me. I could see her there, behind those sea-like eyes. It was almost like telepathy when I heard her voice in my head.

What took you so long? She said.

MERRY

Thursday. March 24, 1977. New Orleans, Louisiana.

I always came to in the same New Orleans drinking place, my journal adrift in a puddle of stale booze. I couldn't recall what happened on those pages. A record of another failed assignment, the words faded before I could capture them. Fleeting images on stained paper, encased in leather. I colored in a few words here and there, before they vanished. Became nothing. A palimpsest of another job already forgotten.

But I always remembered my life.

Two shots should have finished me.

One through the head. The other in my gut.

Some folks said I killed myself in the early morning hours of October 11, 1809. Others were sure I was murdered. I couldn't remember what happened. Someone tore out those pages. Erased those images. Took the final moments that might have given my soul peace.

But the sensational nature of my death did more than destroy my life. It took my chance to finish my journals, to spin my own story, to ensure that Americans remembered me the way I wished to be. Death blocked my view of how people thought of me.

If they thought of me. I didn't know.

I feared my reputation was buried with my remains. As far as I knew, my rotted carcass was shoved into an unmarked grave in Tennessee.

Death led me to Nowhere, a place for shattered souls to perform a good deed for the living, to erase the negative impact of the end of my life and its potential consequences on my immortal reputation.

Could one good deed help me be remembered the way I wished to be?

But my Nowhere was a continuation of my downward spiral, the misunderstandings that haunted the end of my life. I couldn't salvage my name, but failure didn't destroy the urge to try again.

And again.

Until I just wanted Nowhere to end. I craved Nothing.

I blinked. Centuries of embers caught in my nostrils, and fuzzy outlines shifted in the dark. Like every time before, he was waiting on me.

I couldn't recall where I'd been, but I always remembered the Bartender.

"Merry. Knew I'd see you again. What'll you have?"

He showed me his back before I could reply. Me, I rattled the exits, one by one. My sweaty hands slipped off the door handles. Perspiration burned in my eyes. That's what I told myself it was. Tough men, real leaders, we didn't cry.

Just outside, the crowd swayed beyond the cracks in the shutters. Random glimpses of life mingled with my reflection in the wavy glass. Voices drunk with booze and the promise of mayhem. I shouted, but my voice dissolved in the heavy air on my side of the divide.

The Bartender rattled his fingers on the counter. "You know them doors won't open, Merry."

I rested my forehead on blackened stucco. Why did I always fail? Time after time after time? What was next for me? A man with my skills ought to be able to see the way through Nowhere.

How I craved the end.

Resigned, I dragged my fingers across the fog on the window and stumbled back to my seat. It was always mine. Every time.

The Bartender, he stayed in his spot in the back corner. The muscles in his arms worked as he poured the dregs of others down the crusty sink. I squinted into the murk of the place, hoping for some company, some other lost spirit to let me know I wasn't the only one stuck here, the only fool who made this choice.

Glass clinked on glass. "You just missed my last guest. She drank up my top shelf Scotch. Hope you weren't thirsty for that."

"Give me a beer. Draft is fine."

He stopped dumping wet remainders down the drain. Set his amber eyes on me. "Sure you don't want something stronger?"

I scanned the glittering rows of glass bottles on the shelf behind the bar. What mixture might dull the edges of another failure? Whiskey was reckless. Vodka was for the drinker who wanted to disappear into his surroundings. Gin fellows possessed a snooty sophistication I found repellent. Wine-drinking boys were prissy. Draft beer was Every Man.

Every Man wanted to be remembered.

I closed my eyes and imagined myself as an Every Man, not a Nowhere Man.

"Beer's powerful enough."

He made casual work of pulling a foamy pint.

"You want food?" Bubbles frothed onto the sticky wood in front of me as he slid the beer my way. They turned liquid, puddled around the bottom of the glass. I studied my drink and made him wait. Weakness meant letting the Bartender guess what I was thinking.

I picked up the slick glass and downed it in one long draught. Foam sloshed in the bottom when I set it down in a sloppy ring. "I think I'll just get right to my next job. You know I can't abide it here."

Firelight flickered behind his eyes.

"Suit yourself. You got any money left this time?"

I rooted around in my damp jeans, my shirt pockets. In the front slot of my black leather jacket, I found a single note. Crisp. Clean.

I unfolded it slow. Tasted bile. Thomas Jefferson studied me from the face of a two dollar bill. I stared back into those familiar eyes while the Bartender laughed.

"I got new tricks, too. You ain't the only one can change things up."

Glasses crashed into the flagstone floor as I leaped over the bar. When I grabbed him, the front of his shirt was soft in my fingers. "Why is it always goddamn Jefferson? You know he abandoned me, right? At the end? He was happy to let everyone think I killed myself. Never even sent anyone to try and suss out the truth. I worshipped him like a father, and he let me go down in history as the ultimate prodigal son." My voice caught in my throat.

He shook free of me and stepped back, his boots crunching through shards of glass. "I don't make the rules here, Merry."

"Rules. I'll never figure out the rules in this place."

"Hey, don't blame me for your predicament."

My nostrils flared against the stench of spilled alcohol and smoke. Even as I balled up my fist to hit him, I knew he had me cornered. Boxed in. It wasn't his fault I couldn't get things right.

His eyes softened. "You seem to be in a hurry, and I didn't want you to run off without your two. That thing is supposed to be your good luck charm."

"These scraps of funny money haven't made any difference the last seven or eight assignments."

"A dozen, Merry. You're up to an even dozen."

I slumped onto my stool. Thumbed through the pages of my journal. A word here. A scrap of letters there. No hidden message to guide me past the obstacles of Nowhere. To help me avoid the same mistakes. Every Nowhere appearance was new. I couldn't remember them once I failed. Who I met. What I saw. No matter how I arranged what I managed to save from my other outings in Nowhere, I couldn't make sense of the remnants of twelve times tried.

Twelve times failed.

"So, this is number thirteen. Can I just go ahead and skip this one? Have another drink?"

"You been around long enough to know that ain't how it works."

"Goddammit. I know how Nowhere works. I just can't seem to make it work for me."

I closed my eyes and relived the moment Nowhere found me, when I looked into my own dead eyes being covered over with the dirt of a hole that was too shallow to hold me. It was a pauper's burial. An unmarked grave. I was barely cold.

That was when I saw it: a chunk of black leather. It stuck out of the ground at the head of my grave. I pulled it from the dirt, and when I opened it, I read these words:

Remembrance is immortality.
Make people remember your story your way.
Come to Nowhere.

My story was already in tatters. Newspapers trumpeted the supposed details of my apparent suicide. Two men who knew me best—William Clark and Thomas Jefferson—supported that tawdry version of events. Faced with a sensational story, no one cared about the truth.

With one muttered *yes*, I stepped through a portal. Woke up in a New Orleans bar.

The clink of ice teased me back. The Bartender stirred a sulfur-tinged cocktail and pushed it my way. "Seconds aren't allowed, but I'm feeling charitable today."

Liquid heat lit up my nostrils. "What is it?"

"A Thunderclapper. Of all my customers, I thought you might appreciate it."

An homage to the pills members of the Corps of Discovery took for every conceivable ailment. We called them 'thunderclappers' because they gave us the runs. Clark was always partial to them. I had to smile at the memory of him, running off to empty his bowels behind a rock. Afraid he wasn't going to make it.

I raised the glass and sucked the mixture down. Fire ripped through my gullet. Erupted behind my eyes.

The Bartender smirked while I coughed up smoke. "Think of it as a cleansing fire. Erases what's come before." He paused. Leaned his burly frame over the counter and touched my sleeve. "You know this is your last shot, right?"

"Thirteen is my last chance?"

"Yep. You fail this time, you get to be a bartender. Your life will be erased from human history. Nobody will remember you, and what's worse, you won't remember you, either. You get to live forever, though. Slinging booze you can't drink in a room you can never leave."

I looked at his weathered face and wondered who he'd been. What was his story?

How would it feel to forget oneself? To never again close my eyes and see the sun set over the Missouri? To fail to hear Clark's laugh whisper through the trees? To be Nobody?

I wiped my brow with the back of my hand. Whispered my plea. "Tell me. Tell me how to finish this. Please."

He pushed a button on the cash register, and the drawer popped open, a fat wad of bills on one end. He picked it up and tossed it from hand to hand. "I had my own failures, Merry. That don't mean I can remember them. I'm just here to do my good deed. To lubricate your ego a little and send you out again." He stopped and slid the cash across the bar. "This ought to be enough to see you to the end."

"Five hundred? That's too much."

He flicked his eyes to the door. A rattle crescendoed through wood and glass. "Not in 1977, it ain't." He swabbed the bar with a stained towel. "Look, Merry. I got another customer coming. Don't keep making the same damn mistake, all right?"

I grabbed his grimy t-shirt. "What mistake? Tell me."

But instead, he shook free of me. Leaned over and took something out from under the counter. "Here. You lost your hat, and you'll be needing another one."

I looked from it to the two dollars crumpled in my other hand. Jefferson's stare launched me into the streets, patrolling like a lunatic. Searching, seeking the unknown someone who could save me. Rewrite my story. Release me from Nowhere to find whatever was next for a broken soul like me.

And so it began.

Again.

THE THREE R'S OF 21ST CENTURY READING

- **Read** the book - Authors love to sell books, but they really want buyers to read them. If you've come this far, thank you again for reading. Your investment of time matters to me.
- **Review** the book - Amazon and Goodreads don't tabulate book rankings based on sales alone. Reviews weigh heavily into the algorithms for book rankings. Your review matters. More reviews mean higher rankings, more impressions and ultimately, more readers. Please take five minutes and write a review of this book. If you write the review on Goodreads first, you can copy and paste it into Amazon.
- **Recommend** the book - The people in your life value your opinion. If you enjoyed this book, recommend it to five people. Over lunch or coffee. At the water cooler. On the sidelines. Let people see and hear your enthusiasm for this story. Some of them will thank you for showing them the way to a good book.

CPSIA information can be obtained
at www.ICGtesting.com
Printed in the USA
LVOW11s0357100117
520409LV00001B/6/P